A
Strategy
for
Success

A Strategy for Success

by ARI KIEV, M.D.

Macmillan Publishing Co., Inc.

NEW YORK

Collier Macmillan Publishers

LONDON

Macmillan Publishing Co., Inc.
866 Third Avenue, New York, N.Y. 10022
Collier Macmillan Canada, Ltd.

Library of Congress Cataloging in Publication Data

Kiev, Ari.
    A strategy for success.

    1. Success. I. Title.
BF637.S8K45 1977   158'.1   76-55765
ISBN 0-02-563100-4

FIRST PRINTING 1977
Printed in the United States of America

Contents

No ONE HAS the right to say to another fellow adventurer:
Friend, you have lost the way. But each of us has an obligation to ask ourselves—HAVE I LOST THE WAY? Have I
turned my back on what I know to be true and just? Have I
betrayed my own finest instincts? Have I misused God's gift
of body and mind?

—ISAAC EDWARD KIEV
1905–1975

Preface

LIKE MY PREVIOUS guidebook, *A Strategy for Daily Living*, this book has been prepared to help you, the reader, in your efforts to grow, irrespective of the stage of self-actualization you may have reached or the dilemmas you may be facing.

One of my main objectives in writing *A Strategy for Daily Living* was to help people to develop their hidden talents so as to change their lives in a meaningful and rewarding direction. Since the book was published, I have heard from literally thousands of people who have benefited from it and who have come to use it regularly in their daily lives. These exciting results led me to delineate in greater detail the practical steps involved in developing a strategy for daily living so as to help others discover how to improve their lives. The remarkable response to my book, as well as to a series of audiocassette training programs and "The Life Strategy Workshop" which resulted from it, further encouraged me to develop some of the themes in a more comprehensive "textbook" of success strategies.

I have titled this book *Success* because the strategies invariably have proven to be useful in activating hidden talents and energies and facilitating purposeful goal-oriented activity in people from all walks of life.

The significance of developing action-oriented strategies for daily living rests on the assumption that life is not static, that you never reach a "point of insight" from which your life progresses untrammeled by the cares and pressures of the world. Developing life strategies implies the acceptance of change and the recognition of the possibility of preparing for change and adapting your life strategies to changing situations. When you are alive and awake and moving towards a meaningful goal with all your mind and heart and soul, you are in fact succeeding.

"Action and reaction, ebb and flow, trial and error; at the very core of existence, one finds change," wrote Emerson. "Nothing remains the same. Life follows a rhythm. From overconfidence, fear; out of fear, clearer vision and fresh hope. And out of hope—progress."

You may wish, as many do, to prevent change, to conserve the status quo and ensure certainty. If you do this, if you ignore the inevitability of change or vigorously try to preserve the past, you will limit your capacity to adapt to new situations.

Consider for a moment whether in order to avoid making a mistake you must be certain before acting. Has such waiting had serious consequences in the past for you or others? Have you later wondered whether your real error was in assuming that you could anticipate the results of your efforts? Or do you think it is better to adjust as you go along? Can you willingly accept uncertainty, and function despite doubts? If so, you support the view of Oliver Wendell Holmes, Jr., who wrote, "Certainty generally is illusion and repose is not the destiny of man." Ultimately there is no certainty, and each moment contains new possibilities.

At the outset, I would strongly urge you to write down the answers to the following questions; then, as you read the subsequent chapters, refer again to the questions relating to them. The questions and answers will stay fresh in your mind and will help you to think through and to remember the concepts and techniques contained in this book.

Life Strategy Questionnaire

WHAT IS YOUR MOST IMPORTANT GOAL?
WHAT ARE YOUR NATURAL ABILITIES?

1. In what ways does your most important goal relate to your natural abilities?

2. How much time do you spend each day in activity related to this goal? What steps do you take in planning for specific goals?

3. How much time do you spend each day improving your natural abilities?

4. Describe measures you use to master such problems as limited time, multiple commitments, simultaneous tasks, and conflicting priorities, as well as other problems encountered in pursuit of your objectives.

5. Describe how you have reconciled your personal objectives with the objectives of others. To what extent have you consciously pursued an ethic of self-reliance?

6. Under what circumstances have you compromised your ideals?

7. Describe the techniques you have developed to conserve time, energy, and money.

8. What criteria do you apply to resolve conflicting personal needs and the needs of others? To what extent do you put your needs before the needs of others? Under what circumstances do you compromise your needs?

9. How do you reconcile the need for solitude and the need for relationships with others?

10. What philosophical principles or techniques help you to maintain good humor in the face of adversity, conflict, and failure?

Remember: The few minutes you take to write down the answers to the above questions, each of which relates to one of the chapters in the book, will repay you many times over and will increase immeasurably the value of this book for you.

A
Strategy
for
Success

The Power to Change

What makes life dreary is want of motive.

—*George Eliot*

ARE YOU AFRAID of change? Are you unwilling to give up the familiar and take on the unknown? Have you remained in one job longer than you desire? Have you accepted myths about the limitations of your present situation, or are you following a time schedule of your own?

If you are like most people, you probably have never really tested your mettle. The reasonableness and satisfaction of your present life no doubt discouraged change, and you have instead sought to justify earlier decisions by rationalization. A close examination of past decisions in the light of present perspectives may lead to the discovery that your goals and efforts do not relate to your interests or talents, a discovery that may be a step toward freedom. While you may have achieved the goals you set in adolescence, you may no longer be motivated by your original needs yet may be reluctant to take charge of your life. Fear of relinquishing your accomplishments may also prevent action.

You can, if you wish, begin now to do what you now

want to do. This book, a sequel to *A Strategy for Daily Living*, has been written to help you comfortably make the changes you really want to make. It can provide the framework for a personal strategy through helping you develop your own time schedule, so as to overcome myths and standardized notions of reality which can discourage you from pursuing your dreams. This book can assist you in learning how to keep on the track of your own objectives, avoiding diversions which sap your resources, and finally it can help you see how you can resolve most difficulties by focusing on what you can control—your own behavior. To facilitate this, you should become familiar with the various internal and external constraints which limit your freedom. You should learn to apply knowledge gained from past experiences to present ones. Relying on familiar, comfortable routines when dealing with new situations will also reduce anxiety and increase flexibility to develop specific responses for novel aspects of new situations.

To modify your behavior, you will find it useful to understand how your own habitual reactions to others influences your behavior. Most of your actions may really be reactions to others. You cannot change by changing your social environment. You cannot change simply by concentrating on your mistakes and ignoring the positive aspects of your efforts. You can change only if you seek to change yourself consciously, accept responsibility for even the smallest of your own actions, and learn to reward yourself for the smallest increments of progress toward your objectives.

Real freedom comes from knowledge of your needs, of your effect on others, and of others' effects on you. The better you understand your relationship to your social environment, the more you will be able to direct your energies into constructive channels. In effect, you must begin to see the extent to which you assign responsibility for yourself to others, accepting responsibility for them in return, in matters over which you have no control. Once you can see this, you can begin the difficult but rewarding twofold task of giving up control of others and wresting responsibility for yourself from them in areas where you can control your activities.

The capacity to grow comes with time and a minimum effort to control the unfolding of your potential. As Emerson wrote: "Trust the instinct to the end though you can render no reason. It is vain to hurry it. By trusting it to the end, it shall ripen into truth and you shall know why you believe." Your basic ideas have been with you since your earliest years and generally have been reflected in the circumstances in which you find yourself. You can change your circumstances by changing your ideas. Here you must learn to work with perhaps limited but as yet undeveloped resources, since in reality you cannot obtain them from outside yourself. Great teachers recognize this principle and seek not to impose their own views, but to illuminate what ideas their students already possess.

The Power of a Goal

A goal stimulates excitement, energy, motivation, and effort. In fact, the capacity to grow results in part from anticipating and acting in terms of a future goal. Commitment to an idea or goal facilitates concentration of attention and efforts, helps provide the courage to take calculated risks in order to overcome inhibitions and to master fear of failure. The secret of Edison's intensity of effort, which led him to invent not only the electric light but also the phonograph, electric locomotive, microphone, electric pen, and cinematography, was in setting one goal at a time and adapting his life to it.

The greatest satisfaction comes from the fulfillment of your untapped potential, not from fulfillment of tasks set by and rewarded by others. You probably have known exhilarating moments when time flowed smoothly toward some objective. Think back; was this not related to the pursuit of your own goals in your most natural way?

How high should you aim?

You should certainly aim higher than you do ordinarily, and high enough to stimulate your imagination and innovative ability. When people achieve their goals, they may relax and slip into boredom. If you have become bored and unmotivated, it may be that you have reached previously established goals and have not set new ones.

How much effort should you put into pursuing a goal?

Most of us use less than our best effort in pursuing our goals. Fearing failure, we hesitate to commit ourselves fully. Such caution actually reinforces negative expectations, initiating a self-fulfilling prophecy of failure. Success under these circumstances often feels unearned. Failure resulting from partial commitment to a goal will reinforce self-doubt far more than will failure secondary to full commitment, which activates more effort. Ultimately your efforts, not the results provide the satisfaction.

If the magnitude of your goal exceeds your capabilities, you may develop a fear of failure and be paralyzed. Transformation of ambitions into obsessions heightens dependency on others just as increased visibility heightens vulnerability. As William Penn once noted, "The tallest trees are most in the power of the wind and ambitious men of the blasts of fortune." It makes sense then to remember these words of John Burroughs: "Few persons realize how much of their happiness is dependent upon their work, upon the fact that they are kept busy and not left to feed upon themselves. Happiness comes most to persons who seek her least, and think least about it. It is not an object to be sought; it is a state to be induced. It must follow and not lead. It must overtake you, and not you overtake it."

Don't be discontent if you are neglecting important objectives outside your control. Growth occurs most often when you focus on the attainable. Try to concentrate your changes in areas where you have the greatest chance of being able to decide by yourself. Only when you take responsibility for your actions will you genuinely begin to grow.

By concentrating only on effort, not appearance or status, you will master distractions. Plan according to your level of knowledge, seeking to improve yourself by developing your present resources. Assume responsibility commensurate with your position and ability, remembering that Confucius noted that disaster ensued when "weak character combined with an honored place, meager knowledge combined with large plans, and limited powers combined with heavy responsibility."

Seek objectives which challenge and excite you, but avoid excessive preoccupation with results. Try to make the ends fit the means so that you do not seek after something you cannot obtain. As Nehru wrote: "The mere act of aiming at something big makes you big. Strive for great accomplishments, and you will accomplish much, but do not become so enamored of the desire to accomplish that you are enslaved by your own desires."

The distress of ambitiousness derives from impatience in attaining an objective, not from the nature of the objective chosen. Impatience substitutes shortcuts for painstaking effort and leads to dissatisfaction, the anger or envy of others, and, when the objective is reached, feelings of emptiness or unworthiness. Too-vigorous pursuit of a goal may lead to unnecessary competition for and a monopolization of the means to an end. These efforts can distract you. Here power becomes not the means to an end but the end itself, resulting in distraction from realizing your fullest potential, and finally failure to achieve the objective. While fostering intolerance and defensiveness, ambitiousness reduces energy, imagination, and creativity.

Preparation for the Future

Because it magnifies your sense of self-importance, early public recognition can lead to a cessation of growth by fostering antagonisms and complacency. Be cautious. The responses of others can serve as an index of the seriousness of your intentions and as a spur to further efforts to prepare for the future and toward the actualization of your potential.

Fame and power can be traps. Recognizing your talents, others may divert your efforts or sow the seeds of excessive ambition.

Fear of Success

Psychological literature contains much about fear of failure as an explanation for unhappiness, inaction, and persistence in undesirable situations. Fear of increased responsibility, self-determination, and differentiation of oneself from group norms—all characteristics of success—also causes dissatisfaction.

Fear of success manifests itself in lack of risk-taking, conformity, conservatism, rationalization, and an unwillingness to act. While each of us can explain our failures with rationalizations shared by others, we do create the situation in which we find ourselves. Challenging these rationalizations, we recognize the responsibility for what happens to us. Belief in oneself fortifies belief in the achievability of a goal and leads to commitment to the goal. Change requires faith in your beliefs. Self-imposed objectives eliminate limits and give you the power to direct your life.

The Trap of Dependence

Ideas have little value until you translate them into action. Consider for a moment whether you do only what others expect you to do. If you act in terms of your own ideas and goals, you may be able to initiate much that will prove rewarding and satisfying to you.

You may believe that your actions lack originality or that you are merely repeating past actions. Try to approach all acts as if you were doing them for the first time. What you do now will not necessarily be what you did before. Present acts contain ingredients of previous experiences, but more important, they have the power of immediacy, which fosters originality.

Ultimately you define yourself by your actions, not by self-congratulatory or self-demeaning presentations of yourself. As Gandhi once noted, "In the divine account books, only our actions are noted, not what we have read or what we have spoken." The integration of thought and action reduces the conflict between desire and fear, motivation and inhibition, and brings confidence, satisfaction, and results. Screen personalities appeal to us because they seem to transform thought instantaneously into action with a minimum of the inner distress and uncertainty which all of us experience.

Successful creative work results from the transformation of the right amount of thought into action at the right moment. Accepting the natural flow of the universe, you will find that each step prepares you for the next. Ideally, time does not harry the creative person but allows him to realize or actualize his vision.

Perseverance facilitates self-actualization as well as a differentiation and refinement of self. To be creative, you ought not to seek after that which does not naturally flow into you and from you. Learn to accept what happens. Unforeseen events act as correctives, enabling you to get back on the right path. Recognizing the timelessness of the universe, you will be able to concentrate on what you do naturally, eliminating unnecessary activities. Rejecting activities unrelated or irrelevant to your purpose requires conscious effort.

The Right Time to Act

Since you cannot bring about results faster than they can be realized, avoid the inclination to rush into action. Strength comes from patience and the concentration of effort on what you can do. Premature or impulsive attempts to influence results usually backfire.

Planning often requires solitude. Putting your plan into action may require assistance. Watch your timing. You may act too soon because of impatience for a specific result, or act too late because of excessive perfectionism and fear of error.

Each of us possesses unique potential, which relates to our innermost dreams. For this reason, we can best reach our goals only if we follow our own internal logic rather than the logic of experts. If you have known dissatisfaction, it probably has come from failure to do that which expressed your vision. What you fantasize about, what you would do if you had your "druthers," probably approximates the vision you should pursue.

Do you have a concept of how you would like to be in the future? Do you keep to this concept, making efforts to achieve this image of yourself? Do you have heroes that you try to emulate? Who are they? Can you list the five people in the world whom you admire most? If you had three wishes, what would you wish to be? What would you do if you had six months to live? If you had unlimited wealth, on which charities would you spend it?

Learning to express yourself in activity, you will learn what you can and cannot do, and will learn to live in the here and now. Much of the frustration you experience no doubt results from failing to utilize your potential and failing to live according to your inner rhythms.

To live in the present, you must act. This may entail risk if you have to act with insufficient information. You must be open to the experience, to nature, to others, and to yourself. When you listen you must become calm in order to see the uniqueness of situations and your own responses, be they fear or anger or depression. Recognizing your feelings will reduce discomfort and anxiety, and you will be able to act, despite the presence of overwhelming emotion. Thus, you will overcome paralysis.

You must discover the natural rhythm of your own thought processes to develop confidence in the natural expression of your own ideas. While intellectual effort alone will not produce original ideas, relaxation will bring them to the surface. Thus it is that the best ideas often miraculously appear on holidays, when you are free of the daily routine.

The ability to objectify your present situation will help you to modify attitudes that no longer apply, and will increase your capacity to change in the directions you select. By objectifying your situation, you will be able to make better use of your potential and can raise the ceiling you may have set on performance, learning what you can in fact accomplish. Previously conditioned attitudes that may inhibit you from full activation of your potential will be overcome when you learn alternative habits in the mundane routines of daily living.

Preliminary Checklist

Goal: List your important goals. Specifically, list your
    5-year goal
    1-year goal
    3-month goal

1-week goal
Today's goal

At the end of each week consider the following questions:

1. How much time did you spend in activity directed toward your goals during the past week?

2. How much time did you spend doing things determined by others?

3. List those things you are still doing which you no longer wish to do.

Potential

Find where your main roots lie and do not hanker
after other worlds.

—Thoreau

Talent relates to the expression of potential. When we
see true talent expressed, we see honesty, integrity, the
absence of confusion, and genuine openness. Deception and
emptiness repulse us. We shrink from disproportionate presentations of self, from the person who boasts as well as
the person who demeans himself.

How do you know you have talent?

If genuine, talent increases on examination; if false, it
lessens. True talent corresponds with reason, not fancy.
False talent wilts under examination and does not stand the
critical light of day. As John Keats noted, "Beauty is
truth, truth beauty."

Stimulate thought about your hidden potential with these
questions:

1. In what ways do you differ from others in your
favorite activities?

2. In what areas have you had little difficulty in making instant decisions?

3. Describe one activity in which you can concentrate so intensely that you lose track of time.

4. In what activities are you least sensitive to criticism?

5. In what areas do you find people turning to you for advice and opinions?

6. What responsibilities can you readily assume without any anxiety or concern?

7. What recreational activities do you favor?

8. Have you ever engaged in and enjoyed yoga, prayer, physical exercise? Do you practice any of them regularly?

9. How much time can you spend alone without missing others?

10. How much time do you spend daydreaming about what you would like to do?

11. What do you do naturally?

12. What are your special gifts?

13. What do you do well?

14. What do you do comfortably?

15. What magazines do you read regularly?

16. What are your favorite movies and TV shows?

17. List your activities over the past four weekends.

18. What did you do on your last vacation?

19. Is there something others have always suggested that you do which you have repeatedly avoided doing?

The Power of Your Thoughts

Thoughts occur in association with visual images which flow incessantly in both waking and sleeping states. These images motivate action, and most important, you can choose the images you think about. Ultimately you can increase the purpose and energy of your actions by infusing your thoughts with powerful desired images. You can motivate yourself in the direction of your choice.

Understanding the uses of your intelligence, you will be able to recognize and overcome restrictions of habit and environment, and to set meaningful goals. By eliminating egotism and fear of failure, you will be able to take advantage of the enormous untapped resources you now possess.

Decide what to think about. In doing this, you can modify your feelings and your attitudes, in the same way that your feelings may now govern your thoughts.

You can select to focus on thoughts relating to your interests. Try building a list of exciting ideas or stimulating books you have read. Think back to moments when you recounted pleasant experiences, which led you to a positive, confident view of yourself; in these instances, your attitude toward yourself and your ability to think new and exciting thoughts reflected creative thought images.

Since you can decide what to think about, and since you can only think one thought at a time, you can reduce the impact of negative, pessimistic thoughts by focusing on pleasant thoughts. When you next find yourself upset by circumstances and distressing thoughts, concentrate on a pleasant memory that gives you a feeling of serenity. This pleasant thought will improve your feelings, and in turn will add elements of hope and optimism to your present outlook.

Selective Reading

One way to develop your hidden potential, improve your perspective, broaden your vision, and stimulate creative thinking is to read what interests you. Approach reading with a positive attitude. Read only what you want to read. Read vigorously, not passively. Skip about as you read, picking out items of interest. Take notes and consciously review the relationship between your reading and your thoughts. Read at your own pace. Review chapter headings in advance, anticipating what you will find in the book and simultaneously comprehending the entire book. This will make reading more challenging and rewarding.

Think while you read, and keep notes of your impressions. You may find these notes valuable when assessing the extent of your personal growth. Give free play to your curiosity, speculating about your reading.

Trusting Your Instincts

Learn to trust your intuition and follow your hunches. This may resolve more problems for you than logic or intellect. Remember, only you have the answer to the meaning of your life, and you need not seek solutions from others in matters where you and only you may have the answer. Learn when to consult with others and when to work matters out yourself. Don't assume others have better qualifications to determine your objectives or that you cannot develop original objectives. Don't be distracted; don't copy the pace of others who have their rhythms and ways of using time.

Training Your Mind

You can train your mind to function at a level of greater awareness. Studying something new can stimulate you to function in a positive or "plus-24" state, developing highly trained reflexes, much as professional athletes do. Through preparation, new habits, and positive expectancy about events, you will intuitively move toward your goals. By becoming relaxed and undefensive, for example, you can increase your sensitivity to nonverbal communications. You can develop the sense of "reading between the lines," and at times can anticipate events. It is possible, for example, to detect voice changes and body movements which occur in emotional states. To do this you must reduce tension, for tension blocks out stimuli and prepares the body for fight or flight. With training and experience you can learn to relax. This will enable you to receive all available information without reacting to it.

You can learn to control yourself and thus control problematic or crisis situations. In large measure, this involves an awareness of bodily reactions to stress, such as hyperventilation, tachycardia, muscle tension, lightheadedness, and other automatic responses. These reactions can be controlled by learning to breathe slowly and deeply rather than rapidly when in a panic state. Controlled breathing will modify the automatic physiological reactions of panic. Recognition of these physiological responses will help you to master them, and hence to control the major factors motivating precipitous action in a crisis.

Past experiences represent a storehouse of solutions to present crises. Learn to tap your memories to bring your greatest strengths to bear on present situations. Past experiences, dreams, daydreams, and new experiences can provide clues to your potential and your reaction patterns. Risk-taking facilitates growth, the realization of daydreams, and the discovery of suppressed qualities. Regressive mental exercises may create anxiety at first, but can provide you with a greater awareness of your suppressed feelings.

Developing Your Hidden Potential

Knowledge of your weaknesses can be valuable in making choices. If, for example, you shun order, preferring to be easygoing and disorganized, you will be wise to avoid accounting or computer sciences. You may do better in activities that generate excitement, dealing with relatively ambiguous decisions.

Your potential becomes vitalized when you do what you can do, gaining control over your actions rather than responding automatically. You can enhance your potential by relying on yourself and conserving your energies, and by assisting others to realize their potential.

The Value of Achievement

Reviewing successful past experiences can help you discover your hidden potential. Finding links between your efforts and their results can help you determine what can be done and how you might do it. In this way, you can begin to prepare for the future, many components of which will relate to the past.

First, consider whether what you want has been achievable in the past. If not, what must you modify to bring about the desired result? Next, consider the "givens" of your past experience, those inherited or early-acquired characteristics which have influenced your behavior and which no doubt will do so in the future. How have you responded to the stress of disappointment, conflict, and frustration? Consider your range of responses to various life situations. Make mental notes so that you may be able to anticipate ways in which you might respond automatically in the future, and the ways in which you would prefer to respond.

Knowledge: Goals and Potential

Ability and perseverance, not luck or "connections," account for successful accomplishment. Self-discipline, preparation, the improvement of abilities will be recognized when circumstances demand them. When asked, "Who ought to be the boss?" Henry Ford replied, "Who ought to be the tenor in a quartet? Obviously the man who can sing tenor."

Don't minimize preparation or the importance of believing in your abilities. Lack of faith in yourself, manifested by an inclination to minimize your abilities, accounts for the difference between capability and performance. Spinoza, noting this phenomenon, wrote: "As long as man imagines that he cannot do a certain thing, so long . . . is it impossible for him to do it."

By relaxing and controlling nothing but yourself, you can deal with the most complex situations. Problems arise only when you seek specific results by trying to control or manipulate others.

Thoughts produce events. In fact, events are planted in advance in thoughts. What occurs to you, both good and bad, results from your conscious and preconscious thoughts, awareness of which often occurs only in adversity or in the search for achievement or understanding. Explaining circumstances as results of your own thoughts, rather than saying they are due to fate or outside forces, reduces dependency and gives you options to change your life. To overcome difficulties, you need only concentrate on what you have done that may have brought about specific events.

Only effort will increase your strength and awareness of your potential. In time, you may realize that your impact on the world often derives not from what you do but from what you don't do. The ability to control your automatic reactions to stimuli, to control time and space and your movement within them, will give you control over cultural constraints.

In effect, you maximize your capacity to influence the world around you by gaining awareness and control of your automatic responses to the demands of others. By delaying your responses, you can consciously decide how you will act. Action, not reaction, becomes the secret of success.

Think in terms of storing your energy or potential. Look for ways in which you may be squandering your potential by not acknowledging its importance and by allowing it to be drained away needlessly and pointlessly in unconscious activities.

Concentrate on the resources you have, not on those you lack, to develop your potential. Difficult times may develop your resources by forcing you to develop simple, uncomplicated routines rather than self-consciously embellishing or disguising your weaknesses.

To increase your intellectual abilities, you may have to temporarily decrease your attention to emotional needs.

If you accept help from others, do so promptly, so as not to burden them or become so obligated as to affect the freedom in the relationship. If you must ask others for help, do so only after a firm relationship has been established and the request will come naturally. Conversely, in helping others, be alert to the tendency to relinquish yourself. Sacrificing yourself to help another diminishes you, impairs the value of the assistance, and changes the balance of relationships.

In adversity, bide your time and prepare for the future. Study. Don't fight to prove yourself; instead, master the stress inside your head. Prepare for a time of greater opportunity. Preserve energy through patience. This means self-reliance, pursuing what you can now and avoiding dependence on weak people or weak strategies.

Don't stop at the conventional, and don't stop trying to develop yourself. If you sell yourself short, you will give up too soon. Your talents may go unrecognized at times. Use this time to develop yourself and further define your objectives. Your strengths will prove useful in time. Your potential is fundamentally inexhaustible and will be increased as others benefit from you and draw upon you. Unused potential has little significance.

Goal Selection

Far better it is to dare mighty things, to win glorious triumphs, even though checkered by failure, than to rank with those poor spirits who neither enjoy much nor suffer much because they live in the grey twilight that knows neither victory nor defeat.

—*Theodore Roosevelt*

Consider how much time you have in front of you today: days, weeks, months, years, three years, ten years. How do you want to spend that time?

Establish a goal, plan activities today which will enable you to reach that goal, and estimate the time needed to achieve results. If you know your goal ten years from now, you can begin today moving toward it; you will slowly but surely reach that goal by allocating time units to goal-related activities. By differentiating between important and unimportant objectives, you can eliminate activities unrelated to your goal.

I am not suggesting that you become obsessed with your goal, but only that you remain aware of it. A ship's captain has his destination in mind, but concentrates on the work in front of him. Preoccupation with a goal to the extent that you fail to concentrate on immediate activity may lead to efforts to manipulate the outcome; concentration will be on the results of your efforts, not on your efforts. Measure success in terms of your ability to concentrate on tasks of your own choosing, rather than in terms of external factors such as income, prestige, or power. Follow your own track, avoiding the impulse to compare yourself to others. You may learn from watching others, but ultimately you must concentrate on your own efforts.

You can attain your goals and your freedom by setting limits. Unlimited possibilities would overwhelm your life with the boundless. To become strong, you must set limits on your activities and on your efforts by focusing on selected goals.

Regular consideration of an explicit goal will reprogram your subconscious so that you will be guided toward the fulfillment of this goal in the same way that you now move inexorably toward subconscious goals introduced early in life. You can in fact move toward goals you decide upon now instead of those goals established earlier.

Reprogramming your thoughts involves the application of known principles.

1. First, think positively; do not set out to achieve something with a notion of possible failure.

2. If you can visualize the result of your actions, it will help you keep your goals in the forefront of your mind. People are inclined to minimize discrepancies. If you visualize yourself at a certain weight, gradually you will find yourself conforming to this concept. If you visualize yourself as thin, you will begin to experience discomfort when you act in ways incompatible with this image; you will feel less comfortable eating than not eating. There is an unconscious pressure to conform to the image we have of ourselves, which relates to the principle that nature abhors a vacuum. The more you think of yourself in terms of a specific, concrete, desired image, the more your behavior will conform to that image.

In setting an objective, you will naturally begin to act in terms of that objective, without having to engage in complicated avoidance behavior or exercise of will power.

By visualizing the specific image that you wish for yourself, you begin to acquire the habits and attitudes related to it. Acceptance of this image enables you to persist at a task until your performance equals the image. Once again, the principle of minimizing discrepancies holds true.

Ultimately, success involves the conscious establishment of objectives and the conscious implementation of actions directed toward the realization of the visual associated with these objectives.

Much learning also involves reduction of anxiety through conscious review of the facts and circumstances, neutralizing their anxiety-producing properties and providing a broader perspective from which to manage the situation.

Reinforcement of your objectives works best when you think of them in the present tense and in positive terms. Thinking of yourself as already having realized your objectives in the present will reinforce your new self-image much more than if you think of it in future terms. Acting as if you have realized your objectives allows you to become more comfortable with a new view of yourself. It also intensifies your motivation to act in accordance with the new self-image, as well as the power to do those things that go with the image.

Concentration on your objective further reinforces it, and reduces distraction, self-doubts, and negative input from others. Concentration implies an effort to tune out all stimuli that can distract you from your aims.

Concentration requires that you focus on one thing and one thing only at a time. To eliminate self-pity, self-doubt, and excessive dependence on external stimuli requires considerable practice.

Meditation can assist you to draw upon your own internal images, which can be made more prominent than external distractions. Visualizing what has emerged from the innermost recesses of your mind will favor positive results.

While the educational system puts a premium on good

grades, good colleges, and good careers, it provides little opportunity for self-education, self-realization, and the discovery of hidden talents by those who can gain the necessary self-mastery to find themselves in their own efforts.

Beware the "success trap" of looking for your identity in material acquisition. This rarely provides sustained satisfaction. Escalation of efforts to acquire more results in a pursuit of values which may not relate to your needs or deepest desires. Parents who sacrifice their lives for their children often do not benefit their offspring, since such self-sacrifice creates an obligation to fulfill the parents' dreams rather than the children's own.

The modern world drives people on to greater efforts, often in activities that they don't enjoy. Some fail to test themselves in areas of their own choosing, giving excuses about ability, training, lack of experience, and security. When people succeed in a conventional sense but lack happiness, they probably have ceased to pursue their real goal because of fear of failure. A person may involve only a part of himself in activities that interest him so as not to increase his vulnerability, but he may freely take chances in areas of low emotional significance. People delude themselves into believing that they would have succeeded had they tried. They do not realize that they cannot fail when their own interests and natural talents are involved. They can only learn and improve by doing. Failure results when they get off their own track even if they appear to be succeeding by conventional standards. A man who reaches the top of his industry or profession and feels dissatisfied, or feels that he must be constantly alert for fear of losing the position he has obtained, has not really succeeded.

Try improving what you are doing now. Try using what you have. Try observing and listening to the world around you. You may have failed to see what is in front of you. Concentrate on that; don't worry about what you can't see. Above all, recognize the "acres of diamonds" you already possess.

What things have made you happiest throughout your life? How much time do you spend now with what you like most?

List five people you admire and would like to emulate.

List the things you wish had never happened.

List your childhood wishes.

List your adult wishes.

List the compliments you most frequently receive.

By categorizing the contents of these lists you may find a goal related to your greatest interests and talents.

Determining Your Goals

List your present needs and your future objectives; list what you can do to meet your present and future expectations in your work, in your relationships with others, and in recreational activities.

You may, for example wish to work toward a specific job responsibility, skill, or salary level; you may wish to improve certain aspects of your personal relationships; or you may wish to renew your involvement in active sports. In each of these areas consider the steps you must take to move closer to your stated objective, and then consider the following questions:

1. Can the goal be achieved by anyone? Is it humanly possible to achieve the goal, or does it defy the laws of nature? Has it been achieved before?

2. Does the goal conflict with other important goals or with values you cherish? Will pursuit of the goal create conflict for you?

3. Would significant friends and relatives object to the

goal? What support might you expect? Do you anticipate conflict between you and others which would diminish the value of the goal? Are you prepared to deal with lack of support, criticism, or ridicule from others?

4. Have you set the goal high enough to motivate you to action? A goal that is too readily achieved or that has been set by others may not draw your maximum effort, but too high a goal may lead to self-doubt, fear, and paralysis.

5. Do you have the requisite personality traits for achieving the goal, or must you develop them? A salesman should be comfortable talking to people, while a writer should be able to spend considerable time alone. A team player, for example, should be able to put aside personal requirements in favor of a group's objectives. While these characteristics are by no means absolute, it will prove useful to consider such issues when deciding which objectives to pursue.

This kind of self-examination will enable you to determine the extent to which your skills, values, and attitudes relate to your objectives, and will illuminate characteristics you may want to develop. The closer your abilities fit your objectives, the more readily you will achieve these objectives.

The objective should stimulate you to action, regardless of the immediate outcome. Compare the extent to which you are willing to work toward these objectives with the extent to which you have to stuggle and persist despite boredom, frustration, feelings of inadequacy, and the like. Feelings of inadequacy are common, reflecting not so much inadequacy as lack of interest in what you are doing. You are more likely to succeed if your objectives naturally evolve from your basic rhythms.

If you have already staked out your priorities, consider their relationship to your goals. Do they conflict? Are they compatible? You may discover that you are pursuing socially acceptable goals which don't reflect your priorities.

Ask critical questions about goals. Do these goals reflect my interests and values? Am I willing to make these goals a priority activity? Unless your goal is a high priority in your life, you probably will not devote sufficient attention and effort to it to succeed at it.

Ask whether your use of time, energy, and effort relates to use of your greatest resources. Does the use of your resources reflect your priorities? Do you use time and energy in the area of your highest priority? You ought not to simply stop doing what dissatisfies you; you ought to do what satisfies you.

How often do you pursue activities for immediate satisfaction, avoiding the discipline necessary to accomplish a longer-range high-priority objective? How often have you felt the satisfaction of a pursuit requiring self-discipline and perseverance? How much time do you spend in activity unrelated to personal objectives? How often do you put aside your dreams in favor of obligatory daily routines?

To what extent are you giving your goals priority in terms of time expenditure?

Your dreams may be a clue to your innermost yearnings; if you analyze them carefully, you will find recurrent themes in them. Once you accept the validity of your dreams and begin to act to achieve them, you will forget your limitations and bring all your personal resources into play. To renew strength, to reposition yourself, or to find new directions, you will find it useful to reserve time for daydreaming, quiet, contemplation, or prayer. You can walk in the woods or some unfamiliar environment to help break connections with the routine aspects of your life, to gain new perspective. Plan to actualize your dreams and begin to move toward doing this. Once you decide to act, you will discover an amazing source of power within yourself.

If you focus on obstacles, you may become paralyzed, thinking of alternatives and unable to act. The busiest people get the most done, since they do not avoid decisions and commitment in implementing their ideas. Silence will increase the power of your dreams; you will not invite other people's negative views. Others may prove helpful in discussing the processes involved, but not deciding the validity of the objective.

At times, you may want to get help from people who are expert in implementing ideas. State the question correctly. Framing it in terms of feasibility invites unrealistic views of the future. Others may spur you to action by helping you understand your own inhibitions and fear of censure and ridicule. Ask advice on how to get moving, how to overcome inner resistance and external obstacles.

You may want to consider your goals with a close friend, your spouse, or a professional skilled in helping people relate inner needs and resources to external objectives. Many people lack direction and plod along without using their intellectual capabilities to pursue objectives. Consider whether your goals relate to your values, interests, and abilities or whether they represent standardized objectives which actually increase your dependence on group approval.

Do you use the most time for your highest priorities? Do you waste time doing what others could do better? Do you postpone important concerns in favor of less important ones? Is there much conflict between your business commitments and the desire to be with your family?

Beginning

There are twenty ways of going to a point and one is the shortest; but set out at once on one. A man who has that presence of mind which can bring to him on the instant all he knows, is worth for action a dozen men who know as much but can only bring it to light slowly.

—*Emerson*

Change involves the discovery of alternative paths to objectives, using resources in new ways. Most people resist change, acting from habits reinforced by belief in the status quo; they lack a basic knowledge of the steps to take to initiate change. How do you change if you wish to improve your life?

An obvious problem provides a natural stimulus to change. Initiating change in more mundane areas of your life may prove even easier to do.

Record your objective on a 3″ × 5″ card and examine it daily. Verbalizing the goal out loud will add force to your motivation. Don't, however, discuss your goal with others, since this may prove distracting.

Because of the inclination of the mind to reduce the discrepancy between what you believe and what you achieve, the best ways to reach your objectives will gradually come to mind. At the outset, you will find it easier to take nonspecific action rather than detailed steps to reach your objective.

I cannot emphasize enough the importance of paper and pen. Writing down your objectives will make it easier to implement them tomorrow, eliminating decisions about whether or not to do something. In a sense, your list of objectives will give you authority to act, overriding the natural inclination toward self-doubt that is often associated with the start of self-motivated activity.

The Speed of Change

Never plunge into change too rapidly. Move forward slowly and steadily. As problems develop, contain your initial responses. Concentrate on what you wish to do. Proceed with caution and sincerity, focusing on the central issues without modifying yourself to manipulate the outcome. Move slowly, like a coiled spring before it opens. Don't panic or race to escape the crises inherent in change. Try to become familiar with the pressures around you. You can do this best by "not doing," which effectively avoids antagonistic reponses. In this way you free yourself from illusory or false concepts. Remember, persistence underlies success. Never, never give up.

Perseverance will energize your desire to achieve, reduce your fear, and foster confidence in your ability. Perseverance gives a sense of limitless time, which permits you to persist until you reach your objective without rushing to finish, without perfectionistic inhibitions, and without cessation. Through persistence and repeated small steps, continually moving toward your objective, you will eventually gain the power and expertise to reach it. What you believe can be achieved. Accept this idea and you can persist without positive reinforcement.

Recognize your dependence on the universe. Develop active passivity. Accept your limitations, for struggling with them will result in unnecessary loss of energy. To judge a single act too critically is to isolate it and give it too much importance. You must learn to keep moving and not take any one step too seriously. This advice is pertinent, for example, in a situation where you seek to be creative and critical simultaneously. The critical faculty overwhelms the creative drive and produces inhibition, tension, boredom, and apathy. Crises also arise from an ambition to change too quickly. Don't try to rise too high relative to any situation. Find the line of least resistance.

Remain cheerful in the face of adversity and it will be the source of future success. Even if adversity forces you to bend, it will create a power in you which may be unleashed in the future. Don't allow your spirit to be broken by exhaustion in fighting adversity. Be silent, conserve your energy, and avoid new frustrations.

Don't be misled into impetuous action. Wait for the solution to appear. Delay your responses. By doing nothing you can gain strength.

Success results when one combines modesty, adaptability, timing, and activity. Focusing fully on each day, you will not become hedonistic or depressed over the impermanence of things. You may want to pause from time to time and shift directions. Don't ignore opportunities. Don't ask opinions of others fearful of making changes in their own lives; they might discourage you. Seize the day. If you encounter resistance from others, don't argue or try to justify yourself. You will only dilute your force.

As you progress in your chosen direction, be wary of the intoxication of success. At the moment of triumph, be circumspect and sober, and don't overvalue the external trappings of success. Proceed slowly and cautiously, always aware of obstacles which may lurk within and around you.

Progress comes step by step, without assuming the burdens of yesterday and tomorrow. Anxiety relates to an excessive concern for the future, while depression relates to an excessive focus on the past.

Focus on today, proceeding one step at a time. You

will find this difficult if you allow the past to influence you, or if you anticipate criticism which will reinforce perfectionist expectations and the inclination to withdraw if perfection is not guaranteed.

Try to accomplish something each day. Achievement brings satisfaction and strengthens confidence. Achievement results from perseverance, belief in yourself, and a willingness to try without having all the facts. As Samuel Johnson once said, "Nothing will ever be attempted if all possible objections must be first overcome." Actions speak louder than words. You will be judged and tested by your actions, not by your thoughts. While careful deliberation helps, you must ultimately act. Only in this way will you realize your potential. Disraeli once noted, "Action may not always bring happiness, but there is not happiness without action."

To increase your ability and performance:

1. Learn to act immediately upon a decision.

2. Know when to retreat.

3. Use self-motivators—aphorisms, phrases, and other ideas which lead you in positive directions.

4. Recognize the positive characteristics in other people which can assist you and which will help them to improve. This may effectively multiply your effect.

5. Focus on your abilities and successes with neither apology nor boastfulness. Compulsively confessing your faults and failures to others, to avoid criticism for not telling the "truth," results from lack of faith.

6. You may become tense if you don't know when to modify efforts to reach a particular goal. Don't hesitate to change your position in face of stress. Obstinacy, which may keep you from reaching your objectives, results from the failure to recognize that you cannot lose what you have, no matter how much it seems you will. Let go and roll with the punches.

7. You have no cause for anxiety; be patient and let events unfold. Don't plunge headlong into something until the right moment. Try. You will know, when and if you have planned it, when a favorable result is inevitable. But you must first wait and prepare. Misfortune and failure may actually serve as tests of your true desire.

8. To overcome obstacles, you must develop skills for redirecting yourself toward your goals. In the face of crisis, try to postpone action and confrontation until you have something concrete to do.

Step-by-Step Planning

We can easily manage if we will only take each day, the burden appointed for it. But the load will be too heavy for us if we carry yesterday's burden over again today and then add the burden of the tomorrow to the weight before we are required to bear it.

—John Newton

Keep a running list of new interests to explore or skills to acquire. Spend some time each day in studying and pursuing these objectives. This can be the first stage of a long process. Through daily efforts, you build confidence while adding increments of knowledge and skill.

Approaching complex problems in terms of their simplest components can help you to overcome inhibitions and anxieties. New activities will provide the opportunity for hidden strengths to surface, reducing your inclination to act out of habit, and will stimulate new combinations of behavior. Overcoming the unfamiliar, you will experience a sense of mastery. This applies to everything—from learning new languages and visiting new places to testing new wines.

You may have difficulty in finding time each day for new tasks. Try getting up a half-hour earlier each day or cutting short telephone calls, lunch breaks, coffee breaks, and time spent watching television or losing yourself in newspapers or magazines. The search for thirty minutes should be a lesson in self-awareness. You will discover how much time you spend in routines unrelated to your objectives, and how difficult these habits can be to change. You will discover some of the social expectations impinging on your time.

Think of ways to expand your activities or double your productivity. Consider how to use your time more efficiently, working overtime or duplicating yourself by delegating routines to others. Increase productivity by increasing effort. Some activities are more productive than others. Consider whether you spend more time on the least productive activities—those which generate problems, tension, frustration, and minimal results—than on the most important smooth-running and productive ones.

Think of how you can spend more time on productive activity. Although the time-consuming little problems will remain, you can use the best hours of the day for productive work, saving the hours when you have less motivation or energy for the less productive and less important tasks. Unproductive, unimportant activities should be dropped. Necessary routines ought to be delegated, freeing your time for important activities.

A businessman may have more time for new accounts if an assistant handles routines. A housewife can save time by cutting down on telephone chats, combining some activities (TV and ironing, for example), or delegating responsibilities to her children commensurate with their abilities, perhaps affording them opportunities now denied. Letter-writing, organizing bills, knitting, and sewing can be done while watching television. Watching television four hours a day, the national average, amounts to 1,460 hours per year, or 14,600 hours in ten years. Much can be accomplished during that time. Even one hour per day equals 3,650 hours in ten years. You can master Serbo-Croatian,

Aramaic, Sanskrit, or some other complicated language in that period, or even learn to play a Chopin polonaise on the piano.

A mother of two makes something like 16,300 beds in the course of twenty years. Think of the time involved in such routines. To use your time more profitably, you perhaps should hire a housekeeper to do those things which don't require your creative ability. To increase your output, reassess what you do best and most productively.

To gain time for new tasks, find ways of reducing time-wasting routines. Perhaps you spend time going back and forth to the same shopping area. If you plan ahead, you might be able to group activities and save time. Your time might be more efficiently used if you made purchases weekly rather than daily, and arranged for your newspaper, laundry, and milk to be delivered. Reduce your participation in organizations which no longer interest you, and reassess time spent in social routines established in the past.

Streamline your life. Regroup activities in terms of the functions, setup requirements, and people involved. This may save time and, at the very least, will lead you to consider the elements of your activities.

Divide your time into activities, such as telephone time, visiting time, shopping time, and study time. Combine activities according to such a schedule. For example, shop for office and home at the same time. Pick up the groceries on your way to pick up your children from school. This will reduce the time involved in activities such as parking the car, getting a babysitter, or hiring a secretary. Remember activities may be linked by function, location, time, and people.

Devise alternative approaches to your job. Consider new combinations, new times, new locations, new sequences. What would happen if you switched your morning and afternoon schedules? Worked twelve hours a day three days a week, or seven hours five days a week? Worked alone instead of in a group? Worked at home instead of at the office? Perhaps you can produce an item which others can sell, or develop a service relating to your skills or interest. A whole array of activities can develop from your ability to write or sell.

Regular assessment of your activities in terms of their relationship to long-range objectives serves to clarify which ones no longer serve useful purposes and should be eliminated. Extra meetings to supervise others may no longer be necessary; you may want to drop certain courses, even if you will not get a refund. Fear of "losing" money often leads people to continue in redundant activities, or to resume activities that had been postponed, though they may no longer relate to principal interests.

To improve the originality of your thinking, set aside time to acquire new information. Clipping articles and filing them in some organized fashion can prove invaluable. You may find it useful to record new facts on $3'' \times 5''$ cards, periodically examining them until you have mastered the information. Look for ways to use this information in your work. Consider new ideas or activities that might stem from the new information. Development of this personal data bank will put you on top of things as they happen.

Group information by subject. This will increase your command of several areas and help you discover links between disparate phenomena, which in turn will enrich your perspective on the links among your activities. You may find new solutions to certain social or personal problems, and new ways to maximize your resources and your time.

Pursue your tasks on a daily basis. You will monitor changes in them more easily and will increase your chances of reaching your objective. Inability to keep in touch with your activities suggests that you are overextended, and that your efforts will be diluted. You may still be involved in activities long after your motivation has diminished. When you approach projects on a daily basis, you increase the likelihood of success. If you cannot finish all your projects, concentrate on the most important, one at a time.

If you must wait for others or for processing on one project, start the next most important one. Develop a schedule providing sufficient time for necessary routines. Some may require time only once a year, once a month, or once a week.

Develop a master plan for the year which includes the necessary routines, allotting sufficient time for them. Each night, plan the next day's activities so as to increase momentum and ensure some accomplishment.

Keep a list of lower-priority activities that you can turn to whenever you find yourself distracted by the activities of others, tempted to abandon the task, or unsure about what to do. Include some physical activity in your daily routine. Exercise can be both invigorating and relaxing. If it requires concentration, it will also distract you from your problems.

Make a conscious effort to avoid discussion of your goals. Discussions may foster doubt, reinforce perfectionist standards, and invite opposition and criticism.

Try to change old habits. An awareness of the habitual and the innovative will stimulate you to more creative approaches to daily living. The comfort of habit can discourage you from seeking new challenges. In changing habits, you will come up with new and more productive ideas.

Dwelling on inability reinforces self-doubt. Perhaps you have planned to complete something sooner than is possible. Eliminate unnecessary activities; pare down efforts to a reasonable number; hire additional people or delegate authority to others. Avoid discouragement. If you have overloaded yourself, profit from this experience next time.

Raise your expectations as you progress, and establish new goals. You can do this on the basis of past performance. Generate new objectives with new or more complicated tasks, refining what you have done or entering new areas. If you reach your objectives easily, aim higher the next time. New objectives need not be bigger and better, but rather different, novel, or original.

The following checklist summarizes strategies for devising new and creative ways to reach your objectives:

1. Spend some time each day to study and pursue new objectives.

2. Find time for a new task each day.

3. Consider how you might expand your activities or double your productivity.

4. Find ways of reducing wasted time for new tasks.

5. Consider how you can streamline your activity to increase results with less effort.

6. Devise alternative approaches to the job.

7. Consider ways of eliminating some activities while still accomplishing your objectives.

8. To increase originality in your thoughts, set aside regular intervals of time to record new facts.

9. Learn to group facts by subject, and look for connections between apparently unrelated facts.

10. Pursue your tasks on a daily basis.

11. Keep a list of daily objectives or tasks handy so that you can act positively if you get muddled halfway through the day.

12. Include some physical activity in your daily routine.

13. Keep discussion of goals to a minimum, since this dissipates energy and increases vulnerability to criticism when things don't go well.

14. Actively seek to change comfortable old habits.

15. Avoid the inclination to look back at failure, which reinforces self-doubt.

16. Keep raising your expectations.

Daily Efforts

The ability to focus on the present will give you resiliency in the face of obstacles. Concentrate on the issues before you today, not on the unpleasant events of yesterday. All difficulties vanish before the "new interest in the new moment." Taking on more than today's burden will dilute your force and cause fatigue.

Adapt your efforts to your own rhythms. Do creative work at active moments and detail work during slow periods. When your energy flags, switch to activities that will give you more immediate satisfaction. Avoid busywork, but don't assume that you can increase your productivity by delegating the less pleasant parts of a task to others. It may be better to do both the creative and the detailed facets of a task. Absorption in the detailed nitty-gritty may lead to a sense of accomplishment, as well as inspirational thinking. Most great achievements have resulted from one person's pursuit of a dream. Effort leads to self-discovery and a sense of personal power. But don't hesitate to delegate whatever tasks others can do better, giving you time to concentrate on what you do best.

Some people have sudden bursts of energy which enable them to master complex tasks in a single period. Most people must work persistently to gain momentum and to reach their goals. Act without hesitation, and you will not retard your progress by magnifying the obstacles before you.

A change in your routine may upset those who find comfort in the status quo. You must resist the temptation to conform, detaching yourself from expected routines in order to make each day more exciting. Once you initiate change, new opportunities will appear and you will discover enormous sources of power within yourself.

Step-by-step involvement in the present will reconcile the contradiction between independence and the need for social contact. Concentrate on the tasks before you, and these contradictory impulses will slowly develop a harmony of their own. You need not chose between independence and social contact, but can behave according to how you feel at any one time without defining a fixed behavior for all time.

Our technological control over the forces of nature has made us less aware of our vulnerability and the limitations which influence our destiny. Sex, race, age, economics, and temperament, for example, set limits on the expression of our talents. Even the techniques designed for the enhancement of self-expression create limits, just as discipline in order to improve artistic impulses sets limits on their expression. Thus, as you move toward your goal, you risk becoming overly involved with the means to reach that goal—even to the point of losing sight of the goal itself. More commonly, you risk becoming hypnotized by the goal and ignoring the means to get to it.

Concentrate on solutions, not on problems. Concentrate on using your existing resources to develop compatible objectives and strategies. Begin every day fresh, applying your resources to the most important tasks before you. This winning attitude can be developed only by conscious attention to the issues.

Vince Lombardi believed that mental attitude accounted for 75 percent of the ingredients of winning. Everyone wants to win, but most people don't believe they can, and therefore give up before they have tried. The more you believe you can win, the harder you will work. The harder you work, the more you will believe you can win, and the longer you will persist until you succeed.

The most ordinary talents can achieve great feats with persistence, the staying power necessary to keep at something until you have learned it. With persistence you will not be concerned about minor setbacks, frustrations, and errors, but will view them as learning opportunities.

In a sense, then, the most appropriate and satisfactory use of time means concentrating your efforts on what interests you, despite reservations about your ability or the social acceptability of your efforts. Samuel Johnson put it this way: "Few things are impossible to diligence and skill. . . . Great works are performed not by strength but perseverance." Witness Thomas Edison, who conducted 3,000 experiments before perfecting a light-bulb filament. Diligent, consistent efforts give magnitude to the smaller increments. Occasionally, people stop just before succeeding at a task, fearing new responsibilities and new relationships. As Herodotus said, "Some men give up their designs when they have almost reached the goal; while others, on the contrary, obtain a victory by exerting at the last moment, more vigorous efforts than ever before." Often a last-ditch effort adds some mystical increment which could not have been added earlier.

This additional effort may take the form of contemplation, during which time a new solution emerges.

Too often, people miss the opportunity before them, failing to note that a right time to act does exist. Opportunities today may disappear tomorrow. You can't plan for this, but you can prepare for your goal, knowing that the opportunity will arise simply because of your readiness and ability to see new combinations of environmental factors through your unique perspective.

If you stop doing the traditional and habitual, time will become limitless for you. To do this, you must reduce unnecessary activities, including those which may have helped you reach earlier goals but which no longer relate to the future, despite the recognition they may bring you. Don't become too enamored of previous means to achieve certain ends.

Involvement in nonrewarding obligatory activities reduces time, energy, and motivation to pursue your real objectives. Half-hearted efforts, because of insufficient time, discourage further efforts. Success requires time to develop ability and to implement it in tasks you set for yourself.

Planning Your Future

1. How would you plan a day if you had your choice? Prepare an ideal day.

2. Compare this with your actual day.

3. What obstacles prevent you from achieving your ideal day?

4. What skills must you develop to achieve your ideal day?

5. Visualize your life ten years from now. What do you hope to be doing in the following areas: family life, employment, finances, residence, recreation?

6. To what extent are you preparing for your future?

7. What kind of self-improvement program should you develop to make this future a reality?

8. Think of two ways to improve what you do in your job. What academic courses would you take if you had the opportunity?

The Modification of Behavior

There is a tide in the affairs of men which, taken at the flood, leads on to fortune; Omitted, all the voyage of their life is bound in shallows and in miseries. On such a full sea are we now afloat, And we must take the current when it serves, Or lose our ventures.

—*Shakespeare*

Setbacks can provide the stimulus to reassess and redirect energies. All creative efforts include moments of failure. These should be spurs to creativity. Avoid a tendency to escalate efforts rather than shift directions when you encounter an obstacle; escalation can make the obstacle more important than your objective.

Approaching your goals, you may begin to bask prematurely in self-glory or become anxious in anticipation of greater responsibilities. Despite progress, old habits may reappear, taking you off the track. Self-actualization may increase your personal influence or power, which can corrupt when not tempered with knowledge and tolerance, leading to excessive absorption in results without concomitant involvement in effort. Enthusiasm may turn to negativism in the face of new ordeals, and you may become unwilling to commit yourself without a guarantee of success.

Don't take yourself too seriously. Learn to let go; progress cannot be accelerated at will. If you move too fast in one direction, you will have to slow up in other areas of your life. Concentrate on your efforts and try not to compromise yourself. Don't be afraid to stop outdated though successful activities. Focus on current targets.

While destiny plays a hand in all our lives, the thoughtful man, aware of his impact on the people and events around him, can prepare and protect himself. Modesty encourages the support of others more often than does egotism or boastfulness, which foster envy in others. The modest person may seek to achieve great ends but does so naturally. His success seems self-evident and easy.

Great achievements can become difficult if you boast about them in advance. The less said, the better, since this provokes less resistance from others. Because your behavior, not your words, expresses your attitude, be simple and straightforward in a natural way and you will have little opposition.

You can reduce your vulnerability by controlling what you do and say. Don't be pressured by those who consider you mysterious because of your unwillingness to explain your actions to them. Your psychological freedom increases when you have this distance, enabling you to act with less concern over the responses of others, and to observe and listen to the events around you. To delay your responses, you must relinquish your sense of self-importance, which, however gratifying, actually restrains freedom and creativity. This may lead to impatience and intolerance of petty nuisances, but it will help you appreciate events. By controlling your automatic responses to events, you will have a greater opportunity to see them in their genuine form before deciding on your own course of action.

Be alert for the brief instance of opportunity when you can "stop the world" by delaying your responses. You can see the world in moments of transition as changes, especially if you develop observational skills.

You will gain considerable strength by controlling your

accessibility. Otherwise, you will be drained. Approach interactions with some caution—not because of the malevolence of others but to preserve yourself, to avoid exhaustion, and to allow yourself to be more selective. Worry can lead to increased vulnerability and a tendency to listen to those who would encourage constraint.

Avoid discussions which may only magnify your worries. Carefully select those with whom to talk: the knowledgeable lawyer, the experienced friend. Discuss strategies rather than the rightness or wrongness of your intentions. Advice may be helpful in considering approaches to a problem, but must be sought cautiously regarding the decision itself.

In essence, trust your own judgment and free yourself from the tyranny of experts, some of whom you create the very moment you "share" your decisions with them. Keep alert to activities in which others are doing or deciding what you could be doing and deciding yourself. Begin now to make your own decisions.

Logic can help you to explore and organize what you feel intuitively. But don't idolize it as something of greater validity than intuition, or confuse book knowledge with the wisdom which comes from experience.

Serious prayer or even deep concentration can help you reduce your accessibility, since these patterns may inspire reverence, if not awe. Focused activity has a strong impact on others. Even people quietly in motion do not seem subject to uncertainty, ambivalence, and indecision, conveying instead an air of conviction in their efforts and goals.

Concentration on a single objective and confident action toward it inspire awe. Active pusuit of an objective with a minimum of uncertainty and doubt encourages others to pursue their own expectations. Nothing remains the same. When you feel most secure, you are most in jeopardy. If you try too hard to preserve material order in your life, confusion may result. In trying to ensure certain results (status quo), you may lose your grip over them. Be alert to the dangers of security, the uncertainty of material gains, and the changeability of events so that you may avoid the stresses which follow complacency. Try also to balance your capabilities with the situation you encounter. Don't accept a position of responsibility beyond your capability; keep your plans reasonably compatible with your knowledge; and don't assume responsibility without commensurate authority to implement your decision.

Serendipity

Don't ignore the link between preparation and serendipity. Opportunities for great discoveries, inventions, and developments exist in the world but only develop in the minds of those with the intuition, inspiration, or foresight to comprehend the relevance of particular events or circumstances. Newton's discovery of the laws of gravity did not occur simply beause an apple fell from the tree; this event triggered an imagination already conversant with certain laws of physics.

Serendipity, not pure chance, influenced the discoveries of America, penicillin, and the smallpox vaccination. By talking to a milkmaid who believed she was protected from smallpox because of a previous cowpox infection, Jenner conceived of the idea to use the virus of cowpox and later smallpox itself to induce immunity through vaccination. Thus, while searching for a solution, he intuitively seized the chance event and converted it into a significant benefit for mankind. Clearly, preparation plus goal-directedness enhance the significance of mundane events, thereby creating opportunities.

Think Before Acting

All your life your potential has been linked to routines, customs, and obligations which define your role in the world. By learning to delay your habitual responses to the premature expectations of others, you can develop a new perspective and can relate to the world on your own terms. Victories or defeats are merely concepts in your mind. Only actions count. You are not at the mercy of others.

In essence, success requires a definite effort to modify what you've been expected to do. Simply delaying your response may give you a chance to see the constraints others put on your behavior.

Focus your resources on your objectives and avoid circumstances which tax your time and energy. Strength comes from recognizing and circumventing obstacles, avoiding unnecessary suffering or expense. Retreat may allow you to recoup strength and prepare for a comeback at a more propitious time.

Retreating graciously, without rancor or compromise, will fortify your inner strength and give you decisiveness and self-control, which can facilitate subsequent action. By acknowledging defeat, you set limits on its duration and return later with renewed strength. Admitting defeat has less significance than the decisiveness by which you retain control over your destiny.

The Modification of Habits

Biology, past experiences which conditioned certain habits and attitudes, and constant subliminal environmental stimuli limit your present behavior. Understanding the influences of these factors will facilitate your efforts to modify basic habits associated with eating, drinking, and smoking. While changes in eating, drinking, or smoking habits require different specific approaches, the necessary steps have much in common.

One Example: Dieting

Weight reduction is not incompatible with the enjoyment of food. In fact, any suffering or sense of deprivation invariably proves counterproductive. As such, weight reduction programs should seek to maximize satisfaction and minimize distress.

You can in fact learn how to control your eating, which will assist you in beginning a program of weight loss geared to your life-style. You can also learn how you and others in your environment contribute to your weight problem.

During the next thirty days try to do the following:

1. Learn more about your specific eating requirements and habits. To what extent is it absolutely necessary that you follow some prearranged eating schedule which you have followed since childhood—eat precisely at 8:00 A.M., noon, and 6:00 P.M. every day, for example? Think about eating only when you are hungry, and if you can, try this for several days.

2. Learn more about the many useless and harmful notions that you may have aquired over the years with regard to food—for example, the idea that you should eat certain foods at certain times of the day, or the feelings of guilt you may have about eating that force you to always be "dieting" or the dislike you may have of leaving any food on your plate even after you have eaten all that you desire.

3. Learn which of the ever-present food cues presented by advertisements and the like you are inclined to respond to, and take note of your automatic willingness to eat when it is offered to you by people who are eager to offer you food.

4. See whether you can develop a plan of eating around your own life-style and what obstacles you face when you try to reduce your caloric intake. Take note of the times when you are psychologically best equipped to reject offers of food or to reduce your intake, and also note the situations in which your resistance to food is lowest.

Weight loss is directly related to the reduction of caloric

intake below your energy requirements. If you take in fewer calories than you expend, your body will naturally break down some of its stored fat to produce the calories necessary for energy production. The less you eat, the more calories will come from your body and the more weight you will lose. If you eat nothing, you will automatically lose weight. Most people can fast several days each week without any serious effect on their general health.

Overweight, a complication of unnecessary eating, gradually develops from three factors:

1. Social pressure: eating because others expect you to eat, and/or because of reluctance to say no to offers of food.

2. Habit: eating at regular times even when you are not hungry.

3. Anxiety: eating to reduce tension, which is sometimes interpreted as hunger.

You can eat less than you do. Indeed, you may even be able to go several days without food. Recognizing how these three basic causes of overeating operate in you, you will be better equipped to develop a strategy for dealing with each of them.

Too many dieters fail because they do not suit their eating patterns to their own particular needs. The eating patterns you have already established contain the solution to overeating. If you snack late at night, shunning food throughout the day, you will have little success in your attempts at weight loss if you follow a plan which requires you to eat every two hours.

Reducing Social Pressure

Don't tell anyone (except your doctor) that you are testing a weight reduction program. Even when you begin to lose weight and others notice it, do not discuss your diet. Avoid even abstract discussions about food and dieting. Remember how you felt when others were giving you "free advice" about what was "best for you" when you next have the urge to tell someone your "secret" to help them.

If you refuse food offered to you, do so without giving the excuse that you are on a diet. Discussion will only confuse you, get you off the track, undermine your motivation to stick with the program, and reduce your confidence in your ability to master your eating habits. In certain settings, accept the food graciously, but remember, you do not have to eat or drink what is given to you. Try this experiment: for your next five meals, including those you prepare yourself or those you have at a restaurant or a friend's house, leave as much as possible on your plate. Whatever you do, do not clean the plate. It is no more sinful to waste food by dumping it into the garbage than it is to "dump" it into your stomach. This experiment will let you see how much you eat because of social pressures.

You must assume complete responsibility for all that you eat. Do not involve others by asking them to help you evaluate this program. Others will often try to test your strength of purpose. If you want to skip a meal or avoid certain foods, do this without burdening others with the responsibility of your decisions. If you are over fifteen years old, you do not have to explain to anyone why you are not eating certain foods at the "usual time" or, for that matter, why you are eating foods you are "not supposed to eat."

You will have to learn to resist the social pressure to eat when others offer you food or express their "concern" about your noticeable weight loss. Here again, don't discuss your diet or involve others in the preparation of your food, which may start the routine again.

Weigh yourself daily in the morning. In this way you learn, by actual experience, the close relationship between food intake and weight. The object here is to learn the particular pattern of gain and loss that is unique to you and how you can vary your weight by varying your food intake. Each person has a unique metabolism, and you should try to learn about yours by varying the amount and type of food you eat. Only when you have discerned your particular pattern, and have decided how to bring about changes in your weight this way, should you proceed to the next step.

Write down the weight you want to be on a 3″ × 5″ card and begin to think each day for five minutes (without skipping a day) about what you will be able to accomplish at that weight and, perhaps even more important, how attractive you will look.

Developing New Eating Habits

Eat as little as possible each time you have a meal.

Drink as much water, tea, black coffee, and diet soda as possible, even at the expense of eating. Pick two particularly busy days during the week and try to go without food until you experience stomach contractions or true "hunger pains," not simply the anxiety which has led to the conditioned response of eating at "mealtime."

To get around the habit of eating at certain times, try to develop a new set of eating habits. Schedule a pleasant alternative activity for usual mealtimes. The desire for food, which will occur on schedule and lower your resistance, can be overcome by knowing that you will be able to eat later.

To eliminate the "hunger pains," stock up on low-calorie foods, which will temporarily satisfy you and enable you to postpone a heavy meal. This will help you get past the initial periods of hunger, when you often return to your old eating habits.

Overcome the tendency to misinterpret anxiety as hunger. Initially you may need a tranquilizer; consult your physician about this. More constructive ways of coping with anxiety should be developed. It makes sense to begin these alternative activities in anticipation of the anxiety. Once the anxiety begins, try five minutes of exercise or meditation, or do some deep-breathing exercises; if you cannot bring yourself to do this, take a shower.

Suggestions for Reducing Calories

When you do eat, stick to low-calorie food and follow these tips:

Select one type of food—preferably vegetables and fruit, which are particularly good because they are easy to prepare, can be eaten in large quantities due to their low caloric value, and can easily be carried with you everywhere. Restricting your intake to vegetables and fruit will speed weight reduction. More important, it will give you experience in turning down some of your favorite foods, resulting in greater self-control.

You can also select a protein-only diet—i.e., meats, cheese, and other protein foods. But remember, the caloric value of meat is considerably higher than the caloric value of fruit and vegetables. Meat also contains many potentially harmful ingredients, such as cholesterol and fatty acids, and by and large it requires more preparation than do fruits and vegetables.

In any event, if you go on a fruit and vegetable diet, you can eat as much of them as you wish—oftentimes knowing this will help keep you from feeling deprived—although you will lose more rapidly if you eat as little as possible.

Eliminate all starches, grains, gravies, bread, dairy products. Don't think about this; concentrate only on satisfying your needs with as many fruits and vegetables as you can eat.

If you eat out, try to go to the same restaurant every time so that the waiters and waitresses get to know you and can help you meet your particular needs. This will eliminate one of the big pressures to eat more than you need— specifically, the pressure of the waiter showing you a menu and waiting for your decision. People are often embarrassed into ordering too much food or feel reluctant to ask the waiter to remove the bread and butter from the table—a good way to eliminate the nervous habit of filling up on bread and butter before the meal.

1. If you do eat meat, trim off all fat and try to get it broiled.

2. Prepare vegetables without fat. Do not eat creamed vegetables or those prepared in a sauce which contains fat, whole milk, or cheese. These sauces add many calories.

3. Avoid salads containing cheese or whipped cream, and rich dressings with a mayonnaise base, such as Russian, French, and Thousand Island. Italian dressing is probably the lowest-calorie prepared dressing. Oil and vinegar is good, but lowest-calorie dressing of all is lemon or vinegar without the oil.

4. Try to eliminate all fats from your diet. This includes foods high in cholesterol—egg yolk; shellfish; dairy products; baked goods prepared from egg yolk, butter, and whole milk; organ meats (heart, brain, kidney, liver, and sweetbreads)— as well as foods high in saturated fat (animal fats such as lard, suet, salt pork, and bacon drippings). Solid vegetable shortenings should be eliminated. It is better to use polyunsaturated fats or oils (generally fats of plant origin), sometimes labeled "vegetable fat" or "non-animal fat." Most liquid vegetable oils are unsaturated. When buying a new product, check the label.

Eliminate extra fat in the form of gravies, cream sauces, bacon drippings, or butter in vegetables. If necessary, substitute margarine and polyunsaturated fats.

5. Eliminate all bread from your diet. If you feel it is

necessary, you may have Melba toast or zwieback, but without butter. Avoid salty crackers or saltines, which may increase fluid retention.

6. Drink as much water or as many diet drinks as you like, preferably eight glasses of liquid a day. Tea and coffee with powdered cream and artificial sweetener are all right.

7. For dessert, fruit is best. It can be eaten at all times in all situations, even for breakfast. Jello is also good. If you must have ice cream, choose a fruit ice, which has the lowest caloric content.

If you find yourself frustrated and preoccupied with food, go ahead and eat what you want for now, but don't think that at this point you must admit defeat and go back to your old eating patterns. To err is human. Start again tomorrow. Whatever you do, don't broadcast the event to others in order to obtain absolution. They will lecture or scold you or commiserate with you, any of which attitudes will reduce your drive to stay with your program. Your feelings of guilt will help you to get back on the track.

Ways of reducing the caloric intake of certain foods:

1. *Meat.* Choose lean cuts; trim fat; remove skin from poultry; don't add fat in cooking; in roasting or baking, put meat on a rack in a shallow pan so fat can drain.

2. *Breads.* Stick to whole wheat, rye, and white bread, and graham crackers; eat no baked goods except those containing *no* whole milk, fat or egg yolk.

3. *Cereals.* Try to eliminate cereals from your diet entirely.

4. *Dairy Products.* Skim milk; nonfat buttermilk; dried nonfat milk; evaporated skim milk; dry cottage cheese.

5. *Vegetables.* All vegetables except sweet potatoes.

6. *Fruit.* All fruits except avocados.

7. *Fish and Poultry.* These should be used in place of meat when possible.

The Mastery of Stress

A man ought to compare advantageously with a river, an oak, or a mountain. He shall have not less the flow, the expansion, and the resistance of these.

—*Emerson*

Accept your feelings. Efforts to modify feelings lead only to frustration and complications. Patiently examine the nature of your feelings. How long do they last? How long can you tolerate unpleasant feelings? The mastery of stress develops from acknowledging your feelings, not from suppressing them.

You don't require special techniques to increase your awareness. You need only relax and stop doing what you now feel compelled to do to find in yourself what you now seek outside yourself.

Avoiding Anger

The suffering and stress caused by anger often exceed the stimulus which provoked it. Restrained anger hardens into revenge and retaliation, often resulting in remorse. Expression of anger, save in special situations, can lead to irritability, cynicism, and perversity. Whenever possible, try to avoid anger-provoking situations which can blind you to yourself and injure your cause before the world. Such avoidance leads to self-mastery.

Be alert to the tendency to justify your anger; don't ignore its impact on your reasoning power, your effectiveness, and the justice of your cause in the eyes of others. Like drunkenness, anger reveals you to the world while blinding you to yourself. Remember that the medium is the message.

At times the expression of anger can relieve tension and produce a feeling of power, but it rarely proves effective in the long run. Try to substitute more personally rewarding behavior before angry feelings take control.

Rational expression of your distress reduces the danger that resentment and its biological equivalents will build up to unhealthful proportions. Learn which situations to avoid to prevent this buildup of anger.

Opinions and prejudices constitute the basic ingredients of arguments. Since they derive from emotional or nonrational sources, arguments can rarely be "won" on logical grounds. Gentleness, consideration, and understanding of the other person's point of view enhance reasonableness and mutual efforts to discern underlying common interests. Threats to someone's world of assumptions incite defensiveness, regardless of the wisdom of your argument. Tolerance for psychological and physical closeness varies among individuals. Excessive physical proximity or presumptuous statements about cherished values or personality characteristics may be interpreted as aggressive invasions of psychological space.

Agreement has merit only if you don't give up your own opinion and autonomy. Agree to disagree, or agree to avoid conflict, to maintain amicable ties and personal freedom.

Compromise is sometimes necessary. But as Nehru said, "Even when one compromises, one should never compromise in regard to the basic truth. . . . If we always remember the basic objective and always aim that way, it may be possible at a next step to say something much less than that which people understand. But if we forget the basic objective, then the small step may lead us astray."

As long as you are aware of compromising and do so to avoid confrontation, events will proceed. Relationships ebb and flow. Crises slow down in time because discomfort for everyone is induced in sustained conflict. Learn to wait for tension to pass before acting. You may feel justified in acting, through a sense of urgency or self-righteousness, but try waiting a bit longer; neutralize the vengeance of others by your nonresponsiveness.

Goal Selection

Plan major changes carefully. Remember, involving others in your decisions may cause resistance. Most people involve too many people in their efforts, rather than too few. Don't try to justify or explain yourself to others. This puts pressure on you to deal with their positive and negative motivations, and increases the risk of allowing others to take over or to criticize your original plans. As Kipling wrote: "You need not talk about your failures." If others will be affected by your decisions, wait until you have initiated the change before you discuss it with them. However, don't wait until the last minute, since this will often produce negative effects for all.

If you must weigh the pros and cons, the opinions of others and the consequences of your actions, decision-making can be overwhelming. Decisions must often be made with insufficient information. Even "wrong" decisions can overcome inertia and initiate progress toward a goal. To reduce indecision, try concentrating on what you prefer to do rather than on what you believe you should do. This will speed action. Maturity lies in accepting reality, not in demanding perfection. You are not perfect. Your life is not perfect. No day is perfect.

You may suspend time by delaying your reaction. This is a sensible choice, but the illusion of unlimited time may lead to a failure to act at the appropriate time.

Suppression of feelings magnifies their psychological impact. When you suppress your emotional side, you also suppress the power and the "good" within you. Attempting to hide your feelings in anticipation of the responses of others inevitably ends in failure. At the same time, you need not discuss your feelings with others, particularly if you feel they will not treat them with the proper delicacy and consideration.

Only you can decide what to do with your resources. If you do not injure others, you need not be deterred if others feel hurt by your actions or efforts to change. Learn to trust your instincts and be aware of what to bring to bear in a situation.

The more completely you understand your characteristic responses to events, the more accurately you will be able to anticipate your responses in the future. For example, certain characteristics and attitudes toward life in general seem to stem from birth order. First-born children often willingly assume responsibility and yet paradoxically never seem satisfied or certain of themselves. They have inner confidence, yet continually seek to prove themselves. They may strive for approval, yet remain defiantly independent. The second-born, modeling himself after an older sibling, may achieve a better integration of inner confidence and external standards, but may set his sights much lower.

By being between older and younger siblings, the middle child often relates comfortably to both younger and older people—comfortable both as a follower and in taking responsibility for those younger or more helpless.

You may, for example, need to be alone at times, and must reconcile this with your need to be with people. If you were the first-born, you may be able to open up and lose yourself in relationships, but generally will be more inclined towards a deep-rooted conservatism, belying the risk-taking behavior that you may engage in as well. First-born individuals often don't open up to strangers and even occasionally risk isolation in order to maintain their views.

Youngest children may be more charming and helpless. They do not like to be alone, and while superficially confident, may panic in a crisis. Often the youngest seeks support in a spouse or friend, leaning on the other only to find that he or she is dominated by or is competitive with the spouse or friend, who also seeks support of dependent needs.

Thinking along these lines may prove useful, not so much in determining your characteristics but as a way of considering how you relate to others, particularly to peers and the opposite sex. If you apply these concepts to yourself and others, you will be able to understand the underlying patterns of most relationships. Then you will be able to select a life for yourself that may not be too strenuous, for problems in relating to others undoubtedly stem from the psychological predispositions and defenses you develop early in life.

Focusing on the Past

The past provides clues to regularities in your present behavior and attitudes. You cannot relive or undo past experiences, all of which have been encoded in your central nervous system response patterns. But knowledge of past experiences will help you to recognize aspects of your present behavior which you may not have noticed before. Of course, the most critical experiences occur in the first years of life and are least clearly remembered. Nevertheless, the most vivid early memories pertaining to siblings and parents, which occur in the third or fourth year, have much significance, as do later experiences, so the exercise is not entirely futile.

At the same time your present behavior may suggest clues about your past experiences, particularly overdetermined or inappropriate responses evoked by stress. Marked inhibition, fearlessness, and uncertainty may reflect persisting childhood fears, while inaction may reflect self-induced prohibitions. Parents give each child a combination of accurate and inaccurate interpretations of the world, which influence his or her ability to cope with life experiences. These perspectives, transmitted on emotional levels, take fixed form in the subconsious mind and subsequently influence the child's approach to the world.

Adoption of parental values and identification with parents as role models ultimately lead to highly motivated attitudes and behavior patterns. Modeling yourself after a parent who incorrectly perceived the environment, you may have acquired values and attitudes which may not be best for you. You may have been confused by the discrepancy between your parents' words and their behavior. You may even have developed a highly personalized view of the world in order to cope with these discrepancies. This idiosyncratic view of the world may seriously impair your capacity to function.

Parental attitudes have a major influence on your view of yourself. To some extent, everyone develops an inaccurate view of himself from this experience, since the impact of parents on children has more significance for the child than for the parents.

Because one is rewarded for positive and punished for negative behavior, the earliest experiences impart some notion of do's and don'ts in the behavioral sphere. Much behavior remains in a gray twilight zone, since it has been neither rewarded nor punished. Parental conflicts over do's and don'ts may affect your sense of certainty and may produce confusion and a repression of prohibitions, which later may surface in the form of ambivalence and despair.

Rules learned in childhood help develop a sense of

mastery over the environment, so-called reality-testing skills. However, overemphasis on rules may result in failure to develop these skills adequately, which leads to a general lack of confidence and an unwillingness to attempt new things.

The exactness of the rules depends on the nature and intensity of discipline. Parental demands to conform enforced by severe punishment can produce excessive anxiety and lead to subsequent problems. Parents mediate cultural values and attitudes in terms of their own perceptions. They constitute the fundamental source of skills in social adaptation. Even if they are strangers to the language and customs of the culture, they assist children in overall adaptation and psychological integrity.

You may have had parents with a good grasp of the realities of your culture and an intuitive grasp of your needs and capabilities. If so, you learned a style of functioning well suited to later stages of your life. The less reality-oriented your parents were, the more difficulty you will encounter in reconciling your perceptions with those of others.

Television adds visual and auditory inputs to early life experience. Larger-than-life television personalities repeatedly presented in natural emotional tones become important models for identification. Repetitive messages reinforce critical values to be used in deciding between right and wrong, between what ought to be and what ought not to be.

While children consciously discount much of what they see on television, they do not screen out the subliminal cues and role models with which they unconsciously identify. Television reduces the capacity for isolation, and reinforces escapism and passivity and the need for a constant level of noise. It may not be chance that rock music is comprised of a heightened version of this same noise.

Structured situations, or those where you must depend

on others, may evoke feelings and attitudes held toward childhood authority figures. You may transfer old attitudes to new situations and perceive present situations with the perspectives of earliest experiences. Early experiences thus influence perceptions and responses toward others in new situations. If inappropriate to the situation, these responses create conflicts.

In addition to certain internalized rules (conscience) derived from the attitudes of significant others, our fundamental helplessness and dependency during childhood condition a variety of emotional responses in each of us. These emotions color the perception and evaluation of all situations, leading at times to emotional responses, uncanny feelings of guilt and distress, and inexplicable fears.

Guilt feelings also develop in childhood and contribute to feelings of self-hate in both nonspecific and specific situations. Some ambiguous situations evoke feelings of uncertainty, frustration, and abandonment repressed before the age of five by the prohibitions of conscience. The habits and unconscious attitudes resulting from early experiences lead to false perceptions of reality as well as limitations which individuals impose on themselves.

Creative and imaginative attitudes also occur in childhood. Artists skillfully tap these feelings.

The ability to process data from the environment and from internal stimuli also develops during these early years. Processed on a trial-and-error basis, this information assists in the reconciliation of the conflicting demands of conscience, instinct, and environmental constraint. These information-processing skills developed when you began to crawl about and explore your environment. A healthy individual objectively and reliably processes incoming stimuli, and determines appropriate action.

Excessive parental demands or prohibitions can hinder the development of reality-testing ability, prevent a child from acting, or emphasize intellectual development without capacity for action. Warnings and prohibitions may also dampen creative drive. Fearful parents who discourage experimentation stifle reality-testing ability.

Patterns developed in this area influence the perception of reality and the processing of environmental data. Each of us weighs environmental demands in terms of experience, conscience, and previous instruction concerning how to act in a given situation. Growth in these adaptive skills results from experimentation, the imitation of role models, and education.

As a result of negative experiences or parental conflicts in values and attitudes, you may have developed inadequate skills for coping with reality. Overly protective parents may have discouraged you from testing different ways of being or may have usurped certain responsibilities of which you were capable. This may have instilled doubts or fears in your mind, so that you neither tested your skills nor developed strategies to handle various situations. Or you may have developed defensive and maladaptive strategies which were temporarily satisfactory but which may have proved to be counterproductive in later years.

Lack of firm parental discipline may also lead to inadequate development of reality-testing techniques, conflict, and confusion because of difficulty in reconciling the demands of reality. Internalized standards and instinctual drives with fewer preprogrammed strategies make it necessary for the individual to seek new solutions each time to avoid anxiety. Excessive dependency, indecision, or impulsiveness frequently ensue.

Under severe stress, you cannot apply these skills readily. Stress brings out certain automatic patterns of behavior which in childhood may have alleviated distress but which may no longer be appropriate to the adult individual.

Psychotherapy focuses on developing new strategies for coping with a variety of situations. People are helped to develop solutions well in advance of stressful situations by means of conscious techniques and trial and error. A variety of interaction processes assist people in reevaluating various stressful situations and considering alternative ways of coping with them.

Determining Resources from Observation of Your Past

1. In what ways have you changed in the past five years?

2. What one achievement has given you the greatest sense of fulfillment in life?

3. List three statements others have made to you regarding these changes.

4. Have you made plans in the past to move? To change your job? Your marital status? Your financial status? How were you able to accomplish these?

5. How well have you set priorities? A simple test: What has been your most important goal up to the present? How much time have you worked at it, and how much time have you spent in idle conversation, television watching, and the like which has kept you from accomplishing it?

6. How difficult has it been to avoid doing something others expect of you?

7. How well have you been able to keep unpleasant things to yourself?

8. Have you broadcast your achievements to others and then shrugged them off?

9. List the areas of your life in which you have made specific plans.

10. List three areas of your life where you have overcome fears in the past.

11. Describe the most traumatic stresses you have mastered in the past.

12. List the three things you have been most optimistic about.

Alpha States

Autosuggestion can reinforce belief in your goals and reduce self-doubt. One technique involves simply sitting still in a partially darkened quiet room and allowing yourself to submerge to a dreamlike state, while focusing on a key word representing your goal. Another technique, biofeedback, teaches individuals to control their own internal physiological responses with the aid of electronic monitoring equipment.

Yoga, biofeedback, and similar techniques reduce the overload of internal and environmental stimuli, through focused attention generally associated with a characteristic brain-wave pattern (the alpha wave) on the electroencephalogram. The ensuing dreamlike state reduces anxiety and frees motivational reserves which can be used to help overcome impending crises, fatigue, insomnia, phobic and compulsive symptoms, and drug withdrawal. These techniques facilitate concentration and emotional expression and distract attention from distressing thoughts. They enhance recuperation, facilitate objectivity, and increase self-mastery.

The brain can perform calculations and solve other complex problems during sleep. This potential can be tapped to your advantage if you write down problems before bedtime. Relying on the thought processes which continue to occur in the sleep state, you may think through several problems, often awakening with the solution. Sleep often eliminates many secondary thought processes which impede intuitive problem-solving skills.

Western man emphasizes obsessiveness, perfection, and rationality at the expense of emotion and intuition. To overcome the stress of modern life, more emphasis must be given to the emotional side of your brain to get closer to real feelings which govern satisfaction. Dreams and daydreams provide clues to this subconscious side of your personality. Education, with its emphasis on logic and linear thought processes, reduces creative and intuitive types of thinking.

The "isms" found in the modern world have the same effects. Technological endangerment of the environment renders man more inclined to accept ready-made ideological solutions, rather than to search for unique solutions from his innermost resources.

You will accomplish what you expect to accomplish, but you need not evaluate every step in advance, nor should you become too absorbed in your list of steps. Keep your goal in mind. Don't get hung up on your own list; concentrate on it only when you work toward it. Certain goals and activities will stimulate you more than others. Nothing could be more important than these. What you do best is probably the most important activity for you, especially if it comes easily.

Predispositions and attitudes acquired in childhood create limits. For this reason, it is senseless to struggle in areas that result only in frustration. Concentrate on activities you can control, which will be rewarding to you.

Biological and sociological circumstances also create limits. Certain laws of the universe are also limiting. Individual self-expression always encounters obstacles in organizations, families, and schools. The more realistic your view of the social system, the less likely you will be to evoke limiting responses from others.

Efforts to change the world around you may produce unanticipated results. Concentrate only on what you can do, not on changing those about you. Ultimately, your achievement will reflect your efforts.

The notion that more of anything brings happiness leads to overescalation. This in turn leads to dependence on status symbols and possessions, and to a search for security outside yourself. True security comes from pursuing your own inclinations, not from pursuing goals set by others.

The acquisition of "more status" or "more freedom" does not provide greater privileges as long as they depend on decisions made by others.

Reducing Stress

Excessive demands to perform or achieve with minimum effort create stress. The myth of "overnight success" discourages effort at the same time that it escalates standards. The pressure for rapid success creates great stress for those pursuing longer-range goals. The pressure to succeed rapidly generates envy, competitiveness, an increased pace, a sense of urgency, and stress.

To reduce this pressure of simultaneous stimuli, try developing meditative habits, which will enable you to gain some distance from and perspective about your situation so that you can concentrate on the real target and the concrete issues before you. This distancing will enable you to block out erroneous or irrelevant stimuli and to concentrate on your highest priorities one at a time, patiently and silently.

Set yourself at rest before taking action in a crisis, which may overwhelm you with multiple stimuli. Failure to compose your thoughts and establish a strategy or plan of action before acting leads to strife, rejection, and isolation. While you have the opportunity to do so, conserve your energies, build your capabilities, and prepare for the right moment. When you do act, quickly seize the moment. Do not hesitate. Once obstacles have been overcome, you risk serious error if you hesitate.

Should you run from crisis? Probably not. Nehru once wrote that "the person who runs away from danger, exposes himself to the very danger more than a person who sits quietly." Failure to differentiate between your own physiological responses and the external dangers leads to misinterpretation of events. Crises may seem to be external to yourself. You judge something to be frightening if it triggers an accelerated heartbeat, shortness of breath, and a queasy feeling in the stomach. More intense reactions include paralysis of will, tunnel vision, paranoia, and an exaggerated self-consciousness. The intensity of the reaction relates to your own response patterns rather than to the stimulus.

You should rationally assess each crisis in terms of what you can do that might reduce the stress. If you sit calmly, the reaction will subside and you will be better able to assess the situation. When you run, you magnify the fear object in your thoughts.

Learning to Say No

Distasteful choices can be rejected more readily than pleasant, agreeable, and desirable ones. To say no to desirable choices requires more independence and strength and can prove valuable in enabling you to overcome obstacles that impede progress and full self-expansion. If you can learn to stop doing what you don't want to do, you will find it easier to say yes to things that really interest you.

Frustration, defeat, and failure which accompany the crises of change may ultimately lead to success. Character and strength develop from the mastery of defeat. By experiencing failure with its concomitant feelings of depression and discouragement, you will learn that these unpleasant emotions pass in time, and will be less inclined in the future to magnify fear, which can cause more harm than the feared object.

Stress and Crisis

Consider the best moments for retreat and for action. Act in terms of your own objectives, not in terms of the crisis. Bypass obstacles except when you act in terms of duty or a higher cause. Confrontation may prove dangerous and detrimental to those who rely upon you.

The direct way may not be the shortest way. Forging ahead on your own strength may prove hazardous. You may need the support of colleagues to overcome obstructions. If duty calls and you have the experience and inner freedom to act, do so promptly, without becoming caught up in the power of the situation, and return to your routine as soon as possible.

Don't involve yourself in the unintentional transgressions of others. Pass over their mistakes with kindness and understanding, but don't forget that during stress, the best people may avoid you if inadequate people cling to you. You may be inhibited if you adjust yourself to the needs of others. Differentiate yourself, especially from those with whom you no longer wish to be associated.

Adversity may counterbalance prosperity. Adversity stimulates the discovery of inner strengths and interests; prosperity induces laxity and inactivity. The absence of conflict, isolation from others, and a paucity of required tasks reduces motivation. Adversity leads to self-examination, the uncovering of strengths and resources behind the social mask.

By focusing on the positive, you will develop mastery over your fate. This in turn will overcome self-doubt, which can overwhelm you far more than can the actual causes of stress.

Dealing with Negativism

Don't compromise with negativism. The use of force will only weaken you, especially if your actions are negative or repressive. Real security comes from within yourself. Little can be gained by outward displays of strength. A variation of the law of compensation holds that dispersion is followed by in-gathering. If you distribute your goods and services widely, you generate processes of accumulation. The more you give to others, the more will be returned to you. Concentrate on your own development. Others will reconcile themselves to you.

A motivating inner seriousness makes most leaders impervious to external stresses. By understanding and overcoming internal fears, you diminish external threats to small consequence. Avoid comparing yourself unfavorably with others who are experiencing little stress. Focus instead on the potential benefits of your stress.

If your thinking becomes unclear and confused in a crisis, wait until the confusion abates before acting. Frantic pursuit of solutions often creates additional stress. Don't provoke conflict by blaming others. Concentrate on maintaining your own position, warding off unjustified attacks. In dangerous situations calmly look for a safe plateau; avoid involvement if you are not prepared for the consequences.

Always be ready to fully commit yourself when you act. Activity itself will lead to new opportunities and confidence in your ability to become the person you wish to be.

Conscious modification of daily routines can be liberating. Inner strength grows from living in a fluid, unpredictable way. This attitude can eliminate fear. In a crisis, you need neither run nor stand and fight, but rather you can learn to observe and experience the world as it is. You need only live in the here and now. You do not have to act according to past traditions or routines.

The Value of Action

To find satisfaction in your life, seek activity. While action may not always bring happiness, you cannot find happiness without action. Begin to move in some direction whenever you experience distress, regardless of the cause. If fatigue and fear overwhelm you, select easy activities.

Becoming absorbed in the activity will reduce your pre-occupation with distress. Positive thoughts can eliminate distress more effectively than efforts which focus on external causes.

Conservation of Resources

A man may be outwardly successful all his life long, and die hollow and worthless as a puff-ball; and he may be externally directed all his life long and die in the royalty of a kingdom established within him. A man's true state of power and riches is to be in himself, not in his dwelling or position, or external relations, but in his own essential character.

—Henry Ward Beecher

Only you can conserve your income or increase the investment value of your money. The same applies to your time and your energy. Practice prudence, refraining from activities which enervate you and reduce your energy. Life can be enjoyed on material, symbolic, and spiritual levels. Emphasis on instant gratification of the senses reduces recognition of the internal and real world. Excessive spending in ways which reduce your sense of mastery over your own life will make you feel that you lack sufficient money. Money alone does not guarantee freedom or happiness, but distress results if you have less than you believe you need.

Development beyond your present situation requires systematic planning and attention to future matters. But don't allow yourself to be corrupted by the means to achieve economic prosperity. You must control the means— i.e., your own actions. Don't try to control things outside yourself. Adjust to the customary patterns of a particular situation. You can learn from events when you do not try to control them.

Save some fixed percentage, perhaps one-tenth, of all you earn. You will gain satisfaction from this and soon find other ways to save.

Save bits of time, money, and energy. As they accumulate, they will bring you rewards of wealth and freedom. The habit of saving will naturally result in reduced expenditures. Limit your desires. Budgeting will increase your awareness of ways to save. Pay debts promptly. Be content with small gains which accumulate. Don't seek to acquire a fortune through get-rich-quick schemes; such fortunes disappear as fast as they appear.

You can have financial independence if you remain below the standard of living you can afford. Living below your means stimulates consideration of ways to increase gains. Spend time on whatever enhances your earning power. Concentrate on ways to produce more rather than on ways to consume.

Put money to work and build income from savings. Above all, protect your money from loss. Invest in what you know, giving play to your intuition and talent to guide your spending. Results will depend on your use of resources. Daniel Defoe once noted, "All the good things of the world are no further good to us than as they are of use; and of all we may heap up we enjoy only as much as we can use, and no more." Think of this when you find yourself struggling to earn more by working at something you don't like. The accumulation of wealth or possessions which cannot be used is not worth the sacrifices required. Whatever you can use has value. If you can't use something, find out whether someone else might use it. This will prove far more satisfying than you ever imagined.

The nature of reward is linked to the activity you select. Good poetry may lead to literary fame, while business success results in financial rewards.

Beware the pressure of greed—acquiring wealth rapidly is far more difficult than building it slowly. Recognize the virtue of patience and the fact that capital can be accumulated slowly. Wealth can be pursued rationally with perseverance. Probability theory favors slow, sure methods rather than quick ones for the accumulation of money. Match your resources against the amount you wish to accumulate. If you know how much you can earn in a specific time by means of a specific activity, you can calculate the effort necessary to accumulate the larger amount you desire.

Consider:

1. The amount of effort you can and are willing to make.

2. How much present expense you can postpone.

3. How much time you will allow to reach your financial goal. This will allow you to measure the amount of effort required over specific periods of time. To earn more, you must save more, spend less, and/or invest more time earning or learning to earn more in shorter periods. These calculations will assist you to redefine financial objectives in practical, action-oriented terms.

Are you willing to wait several years for the realization of your dreams or for the accumulation of wealth? If you are specific, it will be easier to formulate plans.

It is also useful to calculate the major expenses you anticipate, such as education, health, travel, new business, or retirement.

Consider whether you have negative attitudes toward wealth. Do you feel guilty about accumulating a large sum of money? This attitude results from a failure to think of money as a form of exchange which will increase your capacity to benefit others. Consider also whether you are inhibited by the belief that accumulation of wealth through your own efforts is impossible; this attitude is often due to failure to learn the habit of saving early in life, when one becomes aware of the manner in which money can be accumulated.

Inquire into the simple formulas associated with banking

your money at regular compound interest rates, calculating
how long it will take to accumulate specific sums. It may
take less time than you think. Investment in stocks is another way to compound your money. The greater the
possibility of compounding your money through interest
and dividends, the greater the risk. Here, calculation about
when you want this money becomes critical. Planning for
fixed expenditures in the future will minimize worry and
give you some sense of control over your financial future.

Success without caution can be disastrous. Reaching
your goal, you may encounter problems if you become too
self-confident and fail to set a new goal. Boasting of your
success complicates relationships, generating negative reactions which impede your efforts. Force creates additional
problems. Indeed, the less you apply power outwardly, the
greater the force you will have. If you are a subordinate in
a hierarchy, recognize your position and do not resist it. Be
mindful of the needs and fears of those who have authority
over you. Don't compromise, but seek ways in which you
can express your own talents toward the common good. It
may be necessary to preserve inwardly while yielding outwardly.

In the face of obstacles, keep your objectives to yourself.
Don't arouse enmity by inconsiderate or resistant behavior.
Cooperation will help you to achieve your objectives. Concentration on what you can do alone and most easily may
go further than critical supervision, overbearing kindness,
or taking control. Create a setting or atmosphere and look
for ways to encourage, compliment, and reward. Don't
reward only A work. Praising the efforts of someone who
has failed will encourage him to try harder. The top performers in school, on the athletic field, and in other areas
of life generally work hardest to preserve the standard they
have achieved. Mediocrity results from mediocre efforts,
which reflect one's self-image. To change your own view
of yourself, you must see the relationship between your

efforts and the results. Keep your expectations high and the results will be amazing.

Increasing the Value of Your Ideas

1. To increase the benefits of your own thought and efforts, record your observations of significant experiences. This will be an invaluable future reference, enabling you to compare your present and past reactions.

2. Writing helps thinking and improves personal expression. You may doubt that what you have to say has relevance to others, anticipating the criticism of the insensitive. Or you may think that what you have to say has been said before, forgetting that if it reflects you, it will be unique.

3. Save newspaper clippings. They can be a valuable source of information and a guide to interests, both conscious and subliminal.

4. Your notes and your thoughts have value as information and as a unique perspective developed with the information.

5. By systematically saving thoughts, clippings, and impressions, you increase your fund of information, as well as your familiarity with yourself and with your relationship to various circumstances.

6. By periodically examining your ideas and juggling lists of interests which you may have accumulated, you will find new associations between diverse bits of information, stimulating original ideas. Thus information can lead to new connections.

7. Plan your autobiography in relationship to people and events. Keep a record of experiences in a separate book.

   a. Documents, receipts, notes, photos, picture postcards, and other correspondence should be included.

   b. Keep it sequentially by day, month, year.

   c. Don't compartmentalize it.

By keeping a record of your life, you will give it a special quality, and develop a sense of your own history. Periodic reviews of this book will enrich your life. How often do people look at high school, marriage, and other outstanding early events, and then stop recording their lives? You may unconsciously do desirable things to add to this record, which will enhance your life and assist you to become objective about it.

You will be amazed at how soon you will gain a new perspective on yourself. This autobiographical record will give your life special meaning and make you conscious of how you are living. You will find yourself doing things because they make sense from the script you have been building, even if your motivation for doing it is reduced at the time. Having a record of your life will give you an objectivity about yourself which will facilitate any efforts you make on your own behalf.

People often find themselves doing things on the job that they would never consider doing for themselves. A work assignment provides the justification for and a positive expectation in regard to accomplishment which you could never have for yourself.

You will find an autobiographical record useful when deciding what to do to become the person you wish to be. It will provide perspective and assist you to review your progress periodically, giving you continuity with the past and a view of the common threads in your life.

You will learn to act in terms of a larger vision of yourself rather than one ruled by immediate demands. You will detect areas in which you need to apply some effort in order to provide yourself a rounded sense of self.

Your life can be planned with the same kind of general strategies developed earlier. Your autobiographical record will give you a sense of history, courage, and confidence in your ability to reach certain goals.

Relationships with Others

Friendship is almost always the union of a part of one mind with a part of another; people are friends in spots. This means we cannot simply like someone totally but must accept them as they are, recognizing that they are bound to be limited in some ways just as we are.

—*Santayana*

Friendships can endure throughout a lifetime. Harmonious relationships, characterized by warmth, giving, sympathy, and positive interaction, increase receptivity to poetry, music, and other aesthetic experiences. They also foster courage, making it easier to pursue one's real objectives.

You may differ from others even in areas of shared interest. Discovering these subtle differences can make interaction more rewarding, and mutually stimulating if there is mutual tolerance.

Real friends help you get in touch with your true self. Sharing inner feelings with close friends will increase your perspective of yourself and your objectives. Such communication will reduce misinterpretation, allay anxiety, and maximize openness.

Fear of "hurting" another often masks fear of losing the support of someone believed to be necessary for one's peace of mind. Such negative expectations only magnify fears and bring about the anticipated negative events.

Inhibition of expression, compromise, and resentment may result.

Finding oneself being accepted by others when one behaves openly and honestly with them will invariably foster positive feelings toward oneself and others. Loving relationships generate positive feelings of self as well as stronger feelings of love and affection and positive sympathies toward all mankind.

The Meaning of Love

Love means giving and sharing as well as accepting, and not being stand-offish, defensive, and defiant. In evaluating your capacity to develop relationships, to endure frustration, and to give, consider whether you can admit to biases, prejudices, and weaknesses. Can you accept the loss of a relationship and still persevere, entering into other mutually rewarding relationships?

Openness, honesty, and integrity create strong relationships. Unwillingness to admit to failings or unpleasant emotions generates problems. Fearing rejection, people sometimes hesitate to express the most powerful of emotions—love. This usually stems from a fear that imperfections will be uncovered. Yet the more you can admit your weaknesses to others, the greater will be their capacity to do the same. Ultimately, close relationships require considerable effort at communication.

Affection ennobles and vitalizes, but it can also distort perspective and foster dependency. To maintain the vitality and validity of a relationship, don't take the other person for granted. To do this, you must be able to do without the relationship at times. Periods of solitude apart from the other person preserve individual autonomy, and reduce dependency. Solitude will help you control the inclination to possess or to attempt to change others to suit your needs.

Don't press to initiate or perpetuate relationships, but

allow them to unfold at their own speed. Change and self-renewal enhance relationships, but a conscious effort not to force things to fit prescribed models is often required; allow events to evolve naturally. Similiarly, don't redefine yourself to fit some imagined view of the other person.

Seeking Relationships

Spontaneous relationships have more validity than those based on attempts to curry favor. When dependency develops spontaneously, there is greater freedom of self-expression in the relationship.

In the face of opposition, don't act hastily; wait until matters run their natural course. If misunderstandings arise and someone leaves, don't run after him, for he will only run faster and further away. Wait. Let him return of his own accord. Any attempt to force action fosters reaction. Withstand negative forces and let them disappear of their own accord, rather than generating further hostility by aggressive defense.

Reconciliations occur when natural meetings happen spontaneously. Stick to your gut response in the face of opposition and matters will right themselves. Outcomes cannot be guaranteed. You cannot know the impact of all dimensions of your own behavior, nor all the factors operating in a situation. You can deal only with probabilities.

Have faith. Don't be misled by temporary defeat or obstacles if in your heart you know you are in the right. Retreat gives an opportunity to build up your reserves. Keep to your objectives and you will reestablish yourself on the track again. Don't demand from others what you possess yourself. Don't blame others for your distress or expect them to resolve your problems. This can only weaken you. Conflict often grows from excessive dependency and failure to recognize your freedom to chose.

Be conscious of inconsistencies between your words and your conduct, which lead to similar patterns of inconsistency in those influenced by you.

Balance severity and indulgence, which can foster guilt and the inability to deal with freedom. Don't burden or obligate others through self-sacrifice. When you feel misanthropic, alienated, and irritable, seek support only from those who already support you.

Human misery usually results when we encounter unexpected events unprepared. At times of crisis, people with a natural affinity are drawn to each other as if they had prepared for the eventuality.

If you limit yourself before limiting others, your self-control and chances of success will be increased. Be severe with yourself. Resist temptation and irresolution, and reduce guilt. Behave courteously in formalized relationships. Forbearance toward subordinates and humility toward superiors make sense. In dealing with difficult people, relax in order to increase your empathy with them and discover the best way to minimize conflict and avoid assaults.

Actually, independent people often experience difficulty with the dependent aspect of relationships. Often they maintain an exaggerated view of their own importance to others.

Lasting relationships develop when people share common interests in broad issues, not simply when they share personal interests or dependency needs. Such relationships require effort. Open and honest communication reduces the chances that exploitative patterns will evolve. The open person can more easily invite the participation of others in work toward his objectives.

Prejudice against outsiders can erode positive sentiments within a group. Individuals in the group may begin to distrust one another, fearing the same will happen to them. Low morale initiates efforts to strengthen the group by focusing hostilities on outside groups.

Just as negative attitudes have harmful effects, positive

attitudes can strengthen relationships and bring out the potential within people. Dependency and possessiveness create stress in inexperienced or immature people who are eager to please and to lose themselves in a relationship. The desire to lose one's identity in another person goes back to the inseparability of infant and mother which evolves into separation, individuation, and autonomy. Efforts to sustain a total immersion of self lead to a variety of techniques to escape the distress of conscious thought. The neurotic, unable to become autonomous, seeks mutual dependency in relationships, failing to recognize the "replay" of the infant-mother relationship in the separation anxiety and abandonment of the adult relationship.

People caught in such anxiety-ridden relationships often have a faint glimmer that their distress can be resolved only by reducing the dependency. Fear of losing the positive all-embracing support, however, leads to compulsive clinging or domination. A private sense of self protects against this reaction.

Each person in such a relationship invites the possessiveness of the other by failing to pursue an individual interest apart from the relationship. Sharing all of one's thoughts with another can intensify and reinforce anxiety, possessiveness, and the fear of risking criticism or loss of the relationship by acting independently.

As you change, your relationship will change. To avoid the abrupt termination of meaningful relationships, develop and nurture common interests. Be aware of the tendency to reject those who have qualities you wish to disown in yourself. Recognizing this, you will become more tolerant. Focusing on differences can lead to conflict, recrimination, and subjugation.

Tolerance of differences prevents distress. This applies to the tendency to curtail the freedom of others with the intention of helping them. Genuine support of others means recognizing their individuality and uniqueness, helping them to help themselves. Courtesy and respect for the other person's privacy are critical.

Everyone needs to feel important. This is why people respond when we notice those little things which in their own minds make them unique. The power of kindness lies in its potential for promoting self-confidence in others. As Goethe said, "Correction does much, but encouragement does more. Encouragement after censure is as the sun after a shower." This applies especially to the management of children. It takes courage to allow your children to flounder as they learn how to lead their own lives.

Learning to See the Other Person's Viewpoint

Understanding how others function may reduce interpersonal conflict. To relate to real rather than superficial needs of a critical friend or relative, you must understand that their interpretation of your behavior differs from your own. Perhaps you have reacted defensively, with indirect expressions of dependency which appeared to be authoritarian. Putting aside your needs to improve a relationship can be a positive act rather than a compromise.

Trust. The more confidence you put in others, the more they will act to justify your confidence. By placing confidence in others, you reinforce their importance, instilling a vigor which comes only when someone feels appreciated. The greatest teachers encourage this confidence by taking their students' thoughts seriously. By allowing students to handle errors in their own way, such teachers invite participation and originality. In that the intellect covers a subconscious wealth of resources, it makes sense to encourage others to give their views in matters of judgment, opinion, and attitude.

By initiating the behavior toward others that you wish to see in them, you encourage them to act accordingly. If you want friends, try befriending others, or help other lonely people alleviate their loneliness. If you make some-one happy, you will be happy in turn. If you make someone less lonely, you will be less lonely. Stop thinking about being cared for or about what others owe you. Stop think-ing about what others can do for you. This induces pas-sivity. Instead, do what you can do. Respond to the needs of others. Listen to their stories, problems, and interests. This will in turn increase your own interests.

How to Give Advice

While most people readily give advice, few readily accept or appreciate it. Remember this when next you feel compelled to advise someone, particularly those who have not sought your advice.

When you advise someone, try to do so in confidence, for the presence of a third person may lead you to alter your remarks or embarrass the recipient. Use helpful ex-amples of what you mean in your advice. Avoid criticism, which generates defensiveness and resistance. How you advise often counts more than the advice itself, since the presentation determines whether you will be heard and heeded.

These cautions apply, for example, to relationships with teenagers, who often reject the very advice they seek. Always consider the other person's particular perspectives and limitations. Constructive suggestions presented as ques-tions allow the listener to reach his own conclusions. This protects his dignity as he benefits from your concern and counsel.

Give advice cautiously if you give it at all. Consider how difficult it is for you to take unsolicited advice. If you advise others who do not seek advice, you are being presumptuous and overbearing. The content of a question often counts less than the fact that someone has asked for advice. Perhaps you can respond to this need to ask for help rather than responding directly with the requested answer. People may seek your advice by way of obtaining permission to act in a certain way, shedding some responsibility or even generating praise. You may be disappointed when someone doesn't heed your advice, so consider whether they really want what you offer.

It requires self-discipline to encourage others to help themselves. If you have the confidence and self-discipline it takes to be unpressured by others' demands, they will gain confidence from you through your actions rather than your words. Self-control is difficult when you are being pressured by someone you do not wish to disappoint. Remember that by withholding advice you may transmit to others that they are well suited to determine their own advice.

To accept and benefit from advice requires wisdom. Few people know how to use advice without assigning responsibility for their actions to those who have willingly involved themselves in their affairs. Most of us do not listen to or act upon advice even when it has been obtained from knowledgeable people. If you are reluctant to accept such advice, consider it at a time when you can weigh it against other alternatives. At the same time, don't accept advice through a sense of obligation when it may not be relevant.

Learn to notice more than what you consider important. Record your observations. You may find that you have been missing much about others while thinking about yourself. If you must be a manager in your daily life, as teacher or parent, ask yourself whether you allow others to make their own decisions wherever they are capable. Do you allow them freedom in their work? Do you treat them as unique personalities? Do you understand their need for self-expression and self-determination?

Children, for example, need to be noticed. "Bad" behavior usually stems from this need, not from "bad" character. You can always find a way to be impressed by others. Everyone has something you can like.

Goal-directed action can dispel anxiety and reduce the sense of chaos. In difficult times, be cautious in accepting assistance in matters unrelated to your concerns, for help may obligate you, divert you from your objectives, and limit your freedom to act. But don't categorically refuse help when the right moment comes and you have an opportunity to move naturally toward your goals. It is better to pay attention to this asset than to focus on those things you wish to change.

Self-denial or sacrifice for others imposes burdens on them and rarely proves inspirational or helpful. If you set an example of living freely, your children and others will learn to be free and spontaneous because of their inclination to copy you and because you have not burdened them with your expectations. Trust yourself and others will trust you. Recognize your own need for self-respect and you will recognize the same need in others. Inspiration usually comes best by example, inference, and suggestion, not by command. Most of all, don't interfere, meddle, or dictate to others.

Psychotherapy, sensitivity training, and consciousness-raising groups can heighten awareness of your responsibility and the responsibilities others have for themselves, teaching you to stop assuming responsibility for them.

Acknowledging differences ensures that everyone starts equally in negotiations. This doesn't mean exact reciprocity in everything, but rather that you try to maintain mutual dignity in relationships with others.

Separate issues from emotions, clarifying in concrete operational terms the nature of your expectations and the differences in values.

If you explore common interests and shared activities,

you will be inclined to postpone arguments. Far too often people waste time on useless discussion about unimportant matters. Relegate such issues to lower priorities.

You must overcome the instinctive desire to justify yourself in the face of criticism. Deal with problems by focusing only on what you can control yourself, starting with those activities you do most easily. Be alert also to your automatic or conditional responses to less important matters, which may divert you from your most important objectives.

Don't force results when you encounter obstacles. If you do, you will risk humiliation and defeat. Be patient; forgo immediate results for long-term achievement. In crisis situations, others may confuse and distort the issues. Recognize this danger and proceed cautiously. Only when you feel naturally confident should you move toward your objectives.

Improving Relationships

Relationships deteriorate when people seek to control each other by trying to ensure that present feelings will be preserved in the future. Efforts to perpetuate feelings may lead to hiding unrelated feelings which might be misinterpreted as a lessening of interest. Thus, if you feel otherwise but profess positive feelings simply to avoid offending a loved one, you jeopardize the relationship and stifle spontaneity. You cannot possibly feel the same way all the time. Once you believe that whatever led to the relationship will continue to exist if you allow it to unfold, you will have more security and freedom.

Fear of being hurt often means fear of losing the support of someone you believe you depend upon. When you suppress spontaneity and act contrary to the way you feel, you will experience resentment, which will in turn be expressed inwardly as depression or projected toward others as exaggerated hostility.

Uncertainty and interpersonal conflict generate anxiety. Monitor your impulse to make snap decisions based on acceptance of implicit resolutions of others. Above all, resist the inclination to act on negative expectations which will jeopardize your chances of reaching your goals. If you lack faith in yourself and your relationships, you may unwittingly take steps to bring about the dissolution of a relationship. The self-fulfilling prophecy can spell failure when you become preoccupied with images of disaster in your relations with others.

Jealousy results from fear of losing the support of others upon whom you depend. Jealousy can color your perceptions so that you may misinterpret supportiveness as their attempts to act concerned so you won't be hurt.

Honest and independent concentration on the now of relationships can reduce such anxiety. You can learn to tolerate uncertainty by slowly eliminating ritualistic patterns established to preserve good feelings beyond the present. Such rituals mortgage the present for the future, build resentment, and lead once again to conflict and recrimination.

The Origins of Jealousy

Jealousy constitutes a special case of rejection. Jealousy derives in part from possessiveness, which stems from the universal experience of rejection experienced in socialization.

Jealousy occurs most often where there is intense emotion with strong elements of dependency. The intense involvement renders the individual highly sensitive to the slightest emotional shifts of the other person. This leads to intense positive feelings as well as to irrational rages when the emotional shift is perceived as a threatened rejection.

Jealousy may arise when someone is favored by a parent or boss. If you experience jealousy, review your grievances.

This should lead to the illumination and recognition of various dependency needs and feelings of inferiority. Difficult as it may be to acknowledge these, it will help in the long run to concentrate on changing these qualities in yourself rather than focusing attention on someone else.

If others are jealous of you, try to understand how much may derive from the carryover of dependency needs from childhood. Perhaps you foster these attitudes by flaunting your successes, which suggests that you too may still be motivated by childhood competition and insecurity. By being helpful to those competing with you or jealous of you, you can disarm them, befriend them, and become less defensive.

Envy as a Spur to Growth

Envy, a variant of jealousy, often leads to criticism and fault-finding. If you find yourself criticizing someone, use you own behavior as a clue to your own inner feelings and look for ways to improve yourself, rather than criticizing or copying others. Identify the qualities you envy the most. This may be a clue to an untapped resource in yourself, a quality you may not have developed. Consider what you can do to develop this quality through practice, perseverance, and persistence.

Essentially, by accepting your unpleasant emotions, you accept yourself as you are and put yourself in a position to grow. In accepting negative emotions, you no longer must sustain a false front or defensive posture. At the same time, you are likely to accept others as they are, rather than impose limitations on them when they change. When you impose standards on them, you give them little chance to evolve solutions suitable for themselves.

Change takes time, patience, and effort. Change requires conscious and persistent positive action, not passive acceptance. Change requires responsibility and discipline, not compulsive efforts to act differently by relying solely on techniques or devices which create the impression of growth but which themselves may actually enslave or control you. The more you can see the microscopic dimensions of each behavior pattern that are part and parcel of the activity or behavior that you wish to change, the easier it will be to change. Change can become the hallmark of a life-style, continually propelling you into new discoveries of human potential within yourself. It can induce in you a kindness and magnanimity toward others as well.

Self-Reliance

If I were to try to read, much less answer all the attacks made on me, this shop might as well be closed for any other business. I do the very best I know how, the very best I can, and I mean to keep on doing so until the end. If the end brings me out all right, then what is said against me won't matter. If the end brings me out wrong, then ten angels swearing I was right would make no difference.

—*Lincoln*

The modern world, with all its opportunity for personal growth, creates much self-doubt, uncertainty, and anxiety. Advances in medical technology, improvements in the standard of living, and greater mastery of the environment have led to greater freedom but not to improvements in the individual's quality of life. What is wrong? Did the ancients have greater insight into the means of achieving happiness? I don't think so. But they were more fortunate in having work which required individual effort. This fostered self-reliance. They depended less than we do on decisions made by others in their daily lives. Today, people prepare for a time when others will be sovereign over them in their work. We have little control over sources of food, electricity, and information, upon all of which we depend. More important, we depend on others in matters where we may be better able to make our own decisions, such as work and residence.

The increased population and an apparent scarcity of the jobs, residences, and rewards that everyone wants create anxiety, which initiates a vicious circle of increasing de-

pendence on the opinions of others. Stop accepting the
necessity of obtaining the things you feel you must have.
The moment you begin to live below your means or at a
level where you can maintain control over your life without economic dependency and insecurity, that moment you
gain personal freedom.

Don't discuss your decisions to change with anyone who
has an inclination to resist change. He will prove insensitive
to your desire. Even listening to the "experts" may weaken
your courage to act. This would attest only to your sug-
gestibility; it would not mean that your original decision
was invalid. Sounding out others for reassurance does not
eliminate the anxiety of decision-making. In fact, if you
discuss crucial matters with unqualified people, you may
create more anxiety and confusion for yourself. You have
added their uncertainty to your own.

Many people turn to parents for advice, only to find that
they have re-created childhood patterns of relationships
which may create conflict, recrimination, and dissatisfaction. You must believe in the validity of your own wishes
and desires. Trust yourself, even if all your judgments in
the past have proved inaccurate. Through perseverance,
you will find the right track.

The magnetism of outstanding performers derives from
their total absorption in activity. Their actions relate to their
purposes. They do not seem preoccupied with other matters, nor do they approach their tasks grudgingly. Concentration, persistence, and practice characterize their activities,
which at times seem effortless. Belief in oneself and willingness to make the effort count more than talent. You inherit
talents and develop them through effort. Reliability and
trustworthiness constitute the essence of character, which
develops in relation to other people. While talent and
character can exist apart, it is the person with character
who becomes the leader. Character develops through decision and choices; reputation depends on the opinions of

others. As Mark Twain wrote: "The miracle or the power that elevates the few is to be found in their industry, application and perseverance under the prompting of a brave, determined spirit."

Selecting a Course of Action

In selecting a course of action, consider what Pythagoras wrote: "Choose always the way that seems best, however rough it may be, and custom will soon render it easy and agreeable." Developing new habits makes it possible to change all kinds of things, since they overcome bad habits.

Intellectual habits will increase self-understanding, which justifies your effort and commitment. Knowledge brings a reduction of distress—not necessarily happiness. Ignorance creates uneasiness and anxiety.

Talk to those representing established beliefs which favor the status quo when you want confirmation of a decision to stay put. But remember, unless people have experience with personal change, possess considerable autonomy, and listen skillfully and sympathetically, don't talk to them about your plans which do not favor the status quo.

People with negative attitudes won't encourage you, and those struggling with similar problems may reinforce your doubts about doing what you want. Conversely, action-oriented people may encourage you without listening because of their zeal for action. Avoid talking to gossips, who may spread rumors about your plans. You will know this has boomeranged when inquisitive busybodies offer uninvited opinions. Only someone who can view your problem sympathetically and objectively will help you without influencing you one way or the other in terms of his own situation.

Your self-concept and your world view determines your overall adjustment. Misconceptions about yourself or the world based on outdated attitudes and knowledge will color your perceptions, encourage illusory thinking, and reduce your effort. And fear of humiliation and exposure will lead to further self-doubt, self-deception, and defensiveness.

Recognition of your characteristic behavior can help you gain control of yourself and your life. Understanding the origins of such behavior will facilitate the development of such insight. Inasmuch as your self-concept influences the outcome of your efforts, and inasmuch as you decide what to think of yourself, you can program yourself for success or failure by virtue of the self-concept you adopt.

Assessing Conflict

At times you may be attracted to something you want to avoid. Or you may have to choose between two undesirable or two desirable possibilities. Such choices create conflict, which may in turn stimulate change. Initiating changes which permit self-expression may put the conflict in abeyance and give you a sense of satisfaction. Deciding to change can lead to an assessment of present circumstances, and further stimulus to change if you discover that your present situation does not fulfill your real needs.

Consider how much you have invested in symbols and myths rather than real things. Successful people focus their concerns on getting a job done rather than on the external trappings of their position.

When you try to change, distinguish between changing symbols and changing the real substratum of your existence. Consider where you feel most creative or satisfied. Is it at work or at home, away from the daily pressures of committees, supervisors, or subordinates?

We obtain what we expect from situations. You may only reluctantly stop depending on others to define your identity. Dependency can be very comforting while it also meets the dependency needs of those on whom you depend. When you stop acting in terms of established expectations, you will experience discomfort. This invariably happens when you begin to take responsibility for yourself. Those on whom you have depended may begin to show evidence of their dependency.

Obstacles to Self-Reliance

1. Criticizing yourself to avoid anticipated criticism from others constitutes a major obstacle to self-reliance. Fear of criticism from others can inhibit efforts to take the initiative. Checking things out with others before you act will reduce your sense of responsibility for your actions and your sense of satisfaction in accomplishment. You must of course weigh this against the secure feeling that comes from an activity approved by others.

Discussing the feasibility of your goals with your peers may divert you from your natural interests or may involve you with approaches which do not capitalize on your own resources.

If you invite others to predict the outcome of your efforts, they will do so without accounting for the subtle factors that make for success, such as your willingness to keep going despite failure. Others may assure you that it is okay to stop before you reach your objectives. Such "support" can impede last-ditch efforts to achieve a goal.

Dreams are fragile and ought not to be exposed to either the unsympathetic responses of others, which can discourage effort, or the generous enthusiasm of others, which can turn a challenge into an obligation to perform. Anticipating the responses of others, you may unwittingly try to meet their objections or obtain their approval in your daily efforts. This will distract you from your objectives. You may begin to play-act, to do "the right thing." You may appear to be busy, attending meetings which lead nowhere or becoming excessively fastidious.

At home, you may keep the house so neat as to make it unsuitable for relaxing, or you may feign positive responses to mask negative ones. Unfortunately, the more you suppress, the more you will experience anxiety and fear of losing control. When consciously suppressed, emotions tend to become magnified, leading to more effort to create a conventional impression. Efforts to become self-reliant are minimized by efforts to be accepted and not criticized.

2. Unwillingness to allow yourself to feel good or to act confidently also impedes self-reliance, and stems from fear that others will reject you unless you accept their pessimism or caution about you and act critically toward yourself. This might be satisfactory if you obtained approval from such self-criticism. More likely, such behavior will invite affirmations from others about your negative view of yourself, which can only confuse you further.

Criticizing yourself because of failure to measure up to someone's expectations does not necessarily cut off their criticism. The same principle applies to efforts to meet internalized parental standards. In fact, the more you try to meet any standards other than your own, the more you will build up resentment toward yourself. The self-reliant individual relies on his own standards to judge his actions. This leads to freedom and creativity.

The same is true of any external standards. The achievement of such goals adds little to your sense of self. Recognizing this, you may feel distressed when others praise someone who has attained these superficial materialistic or conventional goals. You need not criticize others or point to the greater validity of your goals. Such "sour grapes" can only lessen your confidence in yourself.

Feeling good about yourself may require the avoidance of opinions people have of you or of other people, the latter being more personal than you may think. Additionally, realistic self-contained goals can be achieved through the cumulative impact of daily efforts, so that you can gain satisfaction from your work each day.

It makes no sense to suffer because of failure to achieve unrealistic goals which cannot be pursued on a daily basis, or which require you to delay acting until you have met the perfectionistic standards of others.

Define what gives you positive feelings and confidence. It may require considerable effort to test your limits and to discover your real potential.

3. Self-sacrifice, justified by custom, loyalty, and friendship, is also an obstacle to self-reliance. Duty and tradition often serve to justify neglect of self and keep others bound to you through their reciprocal obligation to you. To overcome this obstacle, review the ways in which you sacrifice your own interest or neglect to pursue your own objectives. Self-interest does not require you to be boastful, selfish, overbearing, or controlling, but for you to recognize your talents and interests and the validity of pursuing them without waiting for others to do it for you.

Self-sacrifice may mean doing what you cannot comfortably refuse to do. Unwittingly you may draw anger. Doing something you do not really want to do will generate resentment and the obligation of reciprocity, which reinforces dependency on others.

4. Fear of solitude discourages self-reliance because of the belief that it will perpetuate isolation from others. Extreme dependency, which depletes the sense of self, constitutes the basis of this fear. Involvement in solitary activities builds self-reliance and increases your ability to respond selectively to the demands of others.

Shyness and a preference for solitude can help you become self-reliant. You may have difficulty in dealing with the dependency needs of others. An inclination to cooperate simply to be agreeable, a willingness to go along with others, reduces personal strength and self-reliance. Even though you may feel comfortable in solitude, you may not know how to prevent the intrusion of others.

You may be afraid to be alone. You may be tied to the demands of others or feel obligated to explain your time to them. When alone, you may fear that it is necessary to explain your thoughts to others—thereby defeating the value of solitude. It takes time to learn to rely upon yourself, time for practical experiences in building up self-confidence.

Practical experiences in being alone can be traveling alone, eating alone in a restaurant, and other activities which ordinarily might be done with others. A valuable by-product of this is an increased awareness of the people around you, and tolerance for others who may also be experiencing discomfort in similar situations.

5. Excessive efforts to be consistent can impede the development of self-reliance. Must you be consistent? At what point does a shift of plans serve as rationalization for neglecting responsibilities or shirking objectives? A good rule is to allow yourself sufficient time at any activity to decide whether you really wish to continue it. Stick to what you decide to do. Don't feel obligated to persist in tasks carried over from the past. Periodically assess what you really wish to do and what your next goals may be, and set aside time for implementing them. You can shift gears at any time, but allow yourself time to ascertain whether you wish to relinquish an activity.

You may not want to change directions because others may be upset by the shift. You can tie yourself to the past and reduce the faith that others have in your ability to do what suits you best. Thus, your adherence to previously successful behavior patterns can create constraints, particularly if you don't wish to give them up.

An undue investment in the symbols and trappings of power can prove burdensome when economic demands require that you relinquish them. The opinions of others weigh heavily here and add to the discomfort. Ideally, you should have functioned from an inner center of drives and dreams in the past and should never have invested too heavily in external symbols.

If you have been mysterious and suddenly open up, you may find that others harbor various misconceptions about yourself and your activities. Do not accept these notions as indications of things to come, but as a reflection of misinformation.

6. Try to overcome the compulsion to do more than one thing at a time. Such overcommitment generates anxiety and a feeling of not having sufficient time. You may overschedule activities in your eagerness to reach your objectives. Ideally, you should plan for periods of rest and solitude, as well as for periodic reassessment of progress and realignment. Consider also the extent of your omnipotent fantasies reinforced by the dependency of others, which give you a feeling of being special and indispensable. Learn to admit your failings and be willing to relinquish the illusory power assigned to you by others. Allow others to do things for themselves and to share in the credit of joint tasks. This will enable you to concentrate on your own most important issues. Begin to establish priorities. If you concentrate on one thing at a time, you will be encouraged to delegate routine tasks to others.

Mastering the present moment will increase your sense of self-reliance as well as your chances of achieving your objectives without feeling harried. You may have multiple objectives, but focus on only one at any given moment. Like many people, you may try to contain the tasks before you by allocating specific amounts of time to them. Once you establish control over many activities and phenomena, you may reach an equilibrium, at which point you may again experience anxiety because the relative calm may make you feel that you are not accomplishing enough or that there is insufficient challenge. This may lead to further overcommitment. Thus you may fluctuate from being overwhelmed to being understimulated. Ideally, you should be able to strike a balance between the two states. If you find yourself fearful of concentrating on what is before you, ignoring other matters, remember that this state will pass, and so will the urgency to do many things.

Thus you will begin to flow with your own feelings, doing more sometimes and less at other times, without self-doubt or guilt.

7. Trying too hard to order your thoughts may inhibit your thinking. You may even become so anxious about being ill-prepared that you will devote excess energy to organizing and scrupulously planning your thoughts, often becoming preoccupied about leaving things out. You may try to make black-and-white distinctions and may be intolerant of ambiguity and uncertainty. Actually, organization of your thinking may lead to reduced spontaneity, inhibition, and uncertainty.

To cope with this, try absorbing activities which require focused but not planned thought. A good example is skiing, for in order to avoid falling while engaged in this activity, you must concentrate. This involves the processing of information through the brain but not thinking about thinking, an activity which can be highly maladaptive.

8. Seeking permission from others to pursue your objectives invites resistance and an excuse to delay beginning. When you act insincerely or contrary to your instincts for the sake of cooperativeness, your self-doubt will increase. Consider how often you agree with others espousing ideas you don't believe in, and how often you willingly share thoughts which you really prefer to keep to yourself. Such efforts to appear to be someone you are not rather

than to be who you are create conflict and self-doubt. When you act contrary to your inclinations, you automatically inhibit self-reliance.

On the other hand, self-reliance facilitates concentration and independence of thought, and will enable you to do what you choose to do without having to conform to public opinion. Self-reliance will help you overcome obsessions, self-doubt, and excessive emotionalism.

9. An inclination to follow the crowd impedes independent thought. Concern about the opinions of others results in a reluctance to step forward with your unique view of the world and diminishes the confidence so critical for original thinking. The moment you begin to think for yourself, you may find yourself obsessed with what others think; this may cloud your thought processes producing turmoil and loss of will.

Start acting in some direction. Movement itself will eliminate the uncertainty, procrastination, indecision, and anxiety of inertia.

The self-reliant individual focuses on the present, not on the past. He does not overreact to events but awaits their inevitable outcome, focusing only on what he can do at any one time. The key is involvement in activity which draws upon all your resources, letting them flow forth naturally. Such abandonment in constructive activity leads to inspiration. Many seek this feeling of abandonment in alcohol or drugs, which create a semblance of a mystical union with higher powers. War, gambling, and other dangerous pursuits produce similar states of self-abandonment.

Life-Styles Compatible with Self-Actualization

Self-actualization develops best with minimum social activity. Socializing fosters sentiments of affection, tolerance, and understanding which can make you abandon your own realm of thoughts. The less frustration you have in areas unrelated to your objectives, the more you will be able to concentrate on efforts likely to facilitate growth and development.

The absence of cares, however, may prove to be a trap if you concern yourself with the opinions of those who would discourage original activity. The same applies to efforts to find happiness outside yourself. An excessive concern for results, particularly immediate ones, will also stifle creativity and the desire to persevere in the face of obstacles.

A respect for truth increases the ability to withstand adversity. Real strength comes from recognizing that others may supersede you. Let things happen. Don't hold on to the past at your own expense. Avoid identifying yourself in terms of material possessions, position, and the symbols of "success."

Everyone differs in the preference of values which must be pursued. Beware of those who presume to know what is best for you. The risk here is that you may give up what you prize most.

Resist the inclination to justify yourself to others. You should be neither chided for what you do wrong nor overpraised for what works out.

Don't focus excessively on the past to determine what to do. The past can only suggest clues as to what may give you the most excitement and satisfaction. Don't feel that you must keep constant. As Emerson said, "Why should we import rags and relics into the new hour? What you do now ought to hold for now and only now. You need not feel obligated to continue to do it."

Every moment offers the opportunity to begin anew.

You may prefer certainty, but once you recognize the inevitability of change, you will be better able to cope with the present and will not try to fit it into an idealized model of the past. Only by living fully in the moment can you truly learn about yourself and the nature of the world; "so to be is the sole outlet of so to know," said Emerson.

When you read, for example, do so thoughtfully. Know what you are looking for before you start. Avoid the inclination to get caught up with the fascination of words, or to drown yourself in facts without a purpose or a system. By reading with a purpose, you will read more rapidly and retain more of what you read.

Solitude promotes self-actualization by putting you in touch with your innermost thoughts, which differ from the social thoughts produced in company. Take the opportunity to focus on your innermost thoughts next time you find yourself waiting impatiently for a bus or a plane. This will surely reduce your distress. At times you should find a hideaway—with no phones or interruptions—for concentrated thought and effort.

Concentrate on one mental image at a time. To do this, make a conscious effort to avoid talkative, distressed, and conflict-ridden people. When you cannot avoid such individuals, try to be silent until they have expended their thoughts. Do not become captivated or involved with them or even with those whose company you enjoy, for they can distract you when you wish to concentrate. Remember, too, that interest and calmness of mind and body can facilitate concentration. So focus on what interests you and avoid unnecessary movement.

Whenever you resume an intellectual activity, begin with the themes that interested you previously. When your thinking becomes dull and focused on words, conjure up images of real people, events, or situations. This will revitalize your thoughts. Think of examples even if you don't ultimately use them.

Intrusive thoughts may interfere with concentration. These thoughts may be pleasant or negative but often cannot easily be dismissed from consciousness. Close inspection of such obsessive thinking often reveals an underlying fear of failure and an excessive concern for the opinions of others, which interfere with involvement in the task.

These thoughts may also occur in the course of a relationship with others, such as being especially affable to someone you dislike, which generates repressed thoughts and anger. Consider whether this type of circumstance may have preceded your efforts to concentrate.

Writing can help you to focus attention and initiate activity. By writing things down, you reduce vagueness and unwillingness to commit yourself. In writing down your goals, you automatically assume more responsibility.

To improve your focus, record the central theme of your goal on a 3″ × 5″ card and periodically examine it as a reminder to keep on target. Genuine interest increases the incentive to concentrate. Find models for thinking in other areas which may be applicable to your present situation. Consider how well something may be done.

Self-Reliance Checklist

1. List activities you shared with others this past week, dividing the list in two columns: those you wished to do and those you felt obligated to do.

2. List the activities in which you persuaded someone else to do what you wanted to do.

3. List activities that you would have preferred to do alone.

4. List the people you find it easiest to get along with.

5. Which people do you naturally find yourself being friendly with?

6. Do you prefer to keep slightly uninvolved when working with others, or do you find yourself becoming absorbed by the group and losing your identity?

7. Do you overreact to criticism, or are you able to listen quietly while others criticize or rebuke you, moving on without saying anything about it?

8. Are you uncomfortable when people turn to you for advice?

9. Do you willingly assume responsibility?

10. Do you have trouble delegating tasks to others?

11. Do you like everything to be orderly—for example, do you like to do routine things at the same times each day, and do you become upset if you are off schedule?

12. In doing things you have never done before, do you seek permission or advice from others before proceeding, or are you willing to take small risks on your own?

13. Do you take on jobs which are harder than the routine? Do you try to achieve goals over your head?

14. Do you avoid doing things that you don't understand or that you find complicated? How long does it take you to give up on a task?

15. Does fear of criticism or ridicule prevent you from doing what you want?

16. Are you inclined to criticize others, to be "helpful," or do you allow them to fumble so that they may learn more effectively?

17. Do you like to plan everything down to the smallest detail?

18. Do you review past mistakes to try to correct them in the future? How much time do you spend doing this?

19. Do you believe you can determine what is best for you or do you believe others know best?

20. Do you put your interests aside to help others?

21. Do you feel uncomfortable about reaching decisions by yourself?

22. Do you keep at a task even when you become frustrated and feel as though you are getting nowhere?

23. How easily are you distracted by others? What techniques do you use to silently convey to other people that you wish to stop a conversation and get back to what you were doing?

24. Do you have difficulty expressing anger?

25. Do you have difficulty expressing affection?

26. Do you avoid giving advice when asked so as not to make people dependent on you?

27. Do you frequently ask questions of others when you know the answer, or when you should be able to come up with an answer as good as anyone else's?

28. Do you ask advice about decisions before acting on them?

29. Are you afraid of assuming new responsibilities?

30. Are you meticulous, exacting, perfectionistic?

31. Do you enjoy taking risks?

32. Do you like new situations?

33. Do you have trouble saying no?

The Mastery of Time

Chance never writ a legible book, never built a fair house, never drew a neat picture, never did any of these things, nor ever will, nor can it, without absurdity, be supposed to do things which are yet works very gross and rude, and very easy and feasible, as it were, in comparison to the production of a flower or a tree.

—*Isaac Barrow*

Customs and habits and the uncertainty of the future prevent most people from living fully in the here and now, and from responding in new ways to new situations. Thus, most people find themselves caught somewhere between the past and the future, unable to tap the resources of memory or to muster up hope for the future, to make each day exciting and fruitful. In seeking mastery over time, keep in mind Elbert Hubbard's definition of genius: "Genius is the ability to act wisely without precedent—the power to do the right thing for the first time."

You may have failed to accomplish something in the past because you did not devote sufficient time to the activities necessary to complete the task, preferring instead to pursue several things at once to "cover yourself." It is better to give your all to one thing at the risk of failure than to go about that one thing half-heartedly and thereby build in a real expectation of failure. This is so because the feeling of having done all you could will give you a sense of satisfaction, regardless of the outcome. Time spent thinking about what you should have done can be spent more profitably on goal-directed activity.

Chance

How often have you blamed lack of time for your failures? The problem actually may have been failure to decide on the most important objectives and then move toward them first. If you believe you lacked sufficient time, you must try to see how you have diluted your force.

Good fortune and misfortune result from perseverance. The spirit of things (Tao) becomes visible over a duration of time. According to the *I Ching*, the results of single actions accumulate over time and result in good or ill fortune. Doubts which occur after minimal effort may discourage you. You must learn perseverance and the ability to screen out pessimistic influences from those around you. Perseverance enables you to repeatedly return to your central focus, renewing your inner strength despite opposition, failure, obstacles, doubt, and derision. Perseverance wins in the long run.

What is clear and luminous gradually rises. What is murky and solid gradually descends. If you persist long enough, you will surely find your place in the universe. With the passage of time, you will be able to assess the essential features of the directions you have been following and will be able to pursue them more consciously.

Failure to persevere results in failure to implement dreams. Simple routines, chores, errands, and favors done for others distract you from the task at hand. Excessive rumination about a task also deters active implementation of ideas. Too much discussion and planning may invite negative opinions favoring the status quo, which in turn may inhibit innovation.

If you calculate the time spent in effective productive effort, you will find it inversely related to time spent in such planning, thinking, and talking. Most accomplishment results from repeated effort. Many people don't recognize this and often give up too soon, when their efforts don't bring immediate results.

To master time, first determine the answers to several basic questions. You should know, for example, how much of your time is spent in self-determined ways, and how much in ways determined by others. How much time do you spend in personally rewarding activities? Keep a checklist of time expended during a week's activities. This will give you an idea of the extent to which you are in charge of your own time, and may also point to a relationship between this and the satisfaction you experience.

To become fully actualized, you must use time effectively. This will give you a sense of completion. Move slowly and steadily toward your goal on a given day. You must utilize your resources to create an artful life. Just as a book or painting expresses a theme which over the course of the book evolves with new shifts and juxtapositions until a sense of wholeness is reached, time expenditure should follow your rhythms. Don't be distracted or seek to copy the pace of others, who have their own rhythms and ways of using time.

A time-related goal will help you recognize the limits of your time and will let you set priorities. Many things you believe urgent may seem less important when weighed against doing what you may never be able to do unless you start moving now. The very act of setting goals will spark your imaginative powers.

Allocate time to activities that provide the best blend of happiness, which might be viewed as freedom from pain or distress, and satisfaction from being or accomplishing. Minimize distress (dissatisfaction), maximize satisfaction. There are dissastifiers and satisfiers. In preparing for activity, match your time requirements with your interests and natural abilities, considering also potential obstacles and conflicting choices. Are you using the most productive time of day for the least productive activities? Are you depending on others to accomplish your objectives? Do you find yourself waiting for others to get ready or to approve? Are you delegating the most important activities to others?

Persistence

The less you know of the time required by an activity, the more likely you will become frustrated when you fail to get the results you want as rapidly as you want them. Determine the length of time for various activities so as to better plan and handle them. Some things take longer than others to develop. If you knew, for example, how much time Edison put into his experiments, how much time Ford took to manufacture his first automobile, you would no doubt persevere until you reached your objectives.

By roughly approximating the time required to reach a certain objective, you can test your progress.

Failure to consider the dimension of time causes people to abandon activities too soon. They either overestimate their abilities or set too high a goal for too brief a time. If you assess the time available and estimate the time required to finish a particular activity, it will be easier for you to decide to go ahead or to choose an alternative activity.

Perseverance

Stress is often experienced when you do not allocate specific time to various activities all pressing for completion simultaneously. An excess of stimuli or many problems needing solutions at the same time overloads the circuits and creates anxiety and uncertainty. To avoid paralysis, don't spend time on details at the expense of the broader picture, but a failure to consider all factors or an over-hasty action based on immediate impulses can also cause considerable distress.

You may find yourself inhibited or paralyzed by multiple choices. To overcome such inertia, begin at once to act in some way toward your larger objectives. Find the smallest activities that you can comfortably begin now. If you must write a thesis, start with a letter. If you have heavy reading ahead, begin with a newspaper or magazine. You can get into the right frame of mind by initiating the fundamental activity related to the more complex task.

Time seems endless in periods of self-consciousness. Knowing that "stage fright"—a situation-related panic—lasts from ten to forty seconds may reduce your fear and over-reaction to stage fright, thus reducing the tension.

By measuring the intensity and duration of stress you can assess its magnitude. Subjective stresses generally do not last as long as objective stresses. The belief that a situation will be difficult to master adds to the sense of stress. You can prepare to handle stress by measuring the time you will be exposed to it and evaluating the objective implications of the stress. If you can plan your actions, especially knowing that the process will not last long or leave any significant after-effects, you will immediately reduce the stressfulness of your situation. Remember that you increase the duration of any conflict by reacting to it. Conversely, you can reduce the duration of conflict and stress by remaining quiet and waiting for it to pass.

You may wish to shirk activities necessary for reaching your objectives because of antagonism toward them. Here you may find it useful to approach the activity slowly, increasing your involvement by gradually extending the time involved. Approach the task at a time suited to your mood, without regard for conventional requirements surrounding the activity.

You may suspend time by delaying your reaction, but the illusion of unlimited time may lead to a failure to act at the appropriate time.

You measure many things by time; you can master many external situations and change your circumstances by extending this practice to new areas.

The Flow of Time

How much of the time do you live in the future and how much have you structured the present along the line of past plans? Enjoying the present, do you try to perpetuate it by scheduling or structuring your future time, believing erroneously that you will have the same spontaneity that you have in the present? Actually, the present will be more pleasant if you allow it to develop spontaneously and don't structure your time too rigidly. You have to let go and stop planning too rigorously.

Allow the future to unfold. You may enjoy something this minute. You cannot entirely plan how you will be feeling tomorrow, so respond to your inner needs and desires, and go with your intuition. You will be more satisfied and will keep your sparkle. The same pattern may cause you to avoid certain things through fear of what will or will not happen in the future.

How much do you do because of a conviction that something will happen? Do you carry an umbrella and a raincoat if you see one or two clouds? Do you refuse an ice cream cone at five o'clock because you are going to be eating at six and don't want to spoil your appetite? Do you force yourself to sleep with barbiturates in order to ensure that you will be up bright and early tomorrow for some special event? How many restraints like this limit your freedom? How much do you do by habit, not because you want to do it?

You should function without guarantees of future results. Let each day evolve naturally. Rely on a general plan but do not develop an exhausting, frenetic pace. Less satisfaction derives from doing five things at once than from doing one small thing well. The same applies if you seek to gain prestige and power from the works of others. You will not find real satisfaction this way and will seek to build an increasingly larger "empire" in order to preserve your new image, overburdened with the expectations of others.

Supplement your distant goals with effort directed toward short-term goals. How much of what you do relates to goal achievement in the here and now? If you try to directly influence results, you must stop concentrating on causes, stop being fully absorbed in the present, and stop doing what you can do.

This shows up in problem situations where you find yourself rushing through activities in order to get some time free to do what you really want to do. It is better to concentrate now on what you believe to be the most important activity than to postpone it for some vague time in the future.

Conserving Time

Conserve time when solving problems. Fifty percent of the solution to a problem results from defining it; twenty percent from enumerating the facts relating to alternate courses of action; fifteen percent from thinking the unthinkable; and fifteen percent from distancing yourself from the problem. Consider these percentage estimates the next time you try to solve a problem. Don't forget to define a problem or to weigh the pros and cons when searching for a solution. Don't hesitate to think the unthinkable or to distance yourself from the problem. In other words, don't spend too much time worrying about the negative aspects of an issue, which will only magnify the emotional aspects.

Spend as little time as possible worrying or acting contrary to your own best interests. Try to break the problem down into its component parts.

First, define the problem. Weigh the facts available. Allow yourself to imagine the most desirable, even improbable, solutions to it. Then put the problem aside. You will be amazed how rapidly solutions will come to mind, especially after a night of "sleeping on them." In all this, cheerfulness can be an enormous asset. As Carlyle has written: "Wondrous is the strength of cheerfulness and its power of endurance—the cheerful man will do more in the same time, will do it better, will persevere in it longer than the sad or the sullen."

TIME AND RELATIONSHIPS

Time governs relationships. Time determines when to meet someone and measure lateness. Delays in arrival may be interpreted as evidence of hostility. Conversely, early arrivals may express anxiety. Spontaneous and unexpected uses of time may express affection; conflicts may develop from demands on time.

A major source of unproductive time use consists of long-standing dependency relationships, manifested by too much willingness to comply with the demands of others. How can you alter such relationships and get moving? Environmental constraints may influence you to ignore what you can do well in an allotted time period. You must continually struggle against the restraints created by the needs of others, by your own reactions to their subliminal emotional reactions or concern, which may be at cross-purposes to your objectives.

At times you may find it easier to restrain others than to change your own behavior. In this way you don't have to assume responsibility for changing yourself, risking error or criticism, but can put the burden on others. Such behavior borders on authoritarianism, which actually masks dependency.

If this sounds familiar, try modifying those aspects of your behavior which are directly under your control—or which ought to be. Seek out areas of your activities where change will be least disturbing to you and least likely to provoke a negative response from others. Schedule activities so that it is impossible to join in the other relationships simultaneously. Gradual shifts of your time expenditure with others will invariably lead to shifts in the patterns of dependency and to new ways of relating.

Do you spend time in certain mutual activities because of obligation or fear that shifts will have negative effects on others? Have you explained your goal's postponement by rationalizing that you "need more information," that you want to share the decision with someone else, or that you cannot relinquish something which is secure, although unrewarding? If so, you have failed to view your own interests as most important. You may not know what you want, or you may not believe you are entitled to pursue your own interests.

Efforts to help or teach others may mask dependency and may exert control over them.

A delay in reacting can reduce the painfulness of criticism, which hurts more when you try to defend yourself. Next time someone criticizes you, hold back your response for at least five minutes. If possible, write down the criticism. Wait until you are in a good mood to glance at it. If it hurts, put it aside. The constructive part of it may work subconsciously, so that you begin to utilize what was said. Delaying your response to criticism will prevent the negative reaction which produces distress and leads to rejection of the constructive aspects of the criticism.

People probably respond to innate characteristics that you have always had, of which you may have little awareness. It often takes time to discover your most positive attributes.

Focusing on a broader objective than the task at hand will increase your ability to listen to and learn from criticism. You need be concerned only as to whether criticism will deter you from your main objectives. Since this depends on you alone, you need not fear the remarks of others. Just be aware of yourself. Criticism may be a clue to how well you monitor your time. If you use your time to express or harbor anger, you are spending your time on someone else's concerns. Anger breeds resentment and fosters worry and distraction. The frustrations that provoke anger in you may be compared to ocean waves that rock ships. Keeping on target will help you to avoid unpleasant emotions.

Carlyle noted that "it is one of the illusions that the present hour is not the critical decisive hour. Write it on your heart that every day is the best day in the year." Each day provides opportunity for self-renewal. Today's accomplishments, not yesterday's, produce the most satisfaction. What you accomplish today can give you an immediate sense of self-mastery and direction. How can you reconcile yesterday's decision and today's objectives? Planning each day within the framework of general objectives provides one solution to this dilemma. Plan for today, and concentrate on the important objectives of today. Don't let past objectives or methods hold you back when you have moved to new ones. Know how far you can go with something and when to stop, to utilize your resources more productively for present objectives.

With less sense of obligation to past commitments, you can approach completed projects with new enthusiasm rather than compulsively seeking to overcome boredom, fatigue, and other negative emotions which are produced by the burdens of yesterday.

Try to look upon unfinished business as a course of new opportunities, ideas, and resources to pursue present objectives rather than as obligations to fulfill. You should have no more sense of obligation in regard to your own past decisions than to anyone else's decisions for you. You can choose for the present. Past and present interests will be linked.

I SCHEDULING TIME

For one week, prepare a written hour-by-hour schedule of activities for the following day, such as:

8:00	breakfast
9:00	shopping/to office
10:00	meeting/coffee break
11:00	visit, etc.
12:00	lunch

II MONITORING TIME

On a second sheet, record during the day or at the end of the day what you *actually* did during the day.

The purpose of these two schedules is to determine the extent to which your plans coincide with your actual activities.

III EVALUATION OF TIME

1. Do you concentrate on routine first, saving what is important for last? Do you have time to do what you want to do?

2. In which areas of your life do you schedule your time most carefully? Accurately? How well do you keep to this schedule?

3. How much free time do you have each day, counting even the scattered brief periods between chores or assignments?

4. Does your schedule create problems in terms of

conflicting activities or insufficient time for specific activities?

5. How much time do you spend on the telephone, visiting, etc.?

6. How important are other people in determining how you actually spend your time?

7. How often do you become bogged down by your schedule when you have lost interest in an activity or wish to proceed to another?

8. Do you sometimes try to do more than one thing at a time? What things?

9. Do you visualize what you wish to do next as you near the completion of an activity?

10. Does your schedule include activities that you can accomplish?

11. Does your schedule include activities that challenge you? Frustrate you?

12. Review the week's schedule and make a list of all of the activities you planned which:

    a. You did not accomplish.

    b. You would have preferred to have left off the list.

13. Calculate the amount of time spent in activities you would prefer to eliminate.

14. Make a list of these activities and reasons why you cannot reduce or eliminate them.

DAILY CHECKLIST

A. Seek to take time from useless projects and idle conversations. Consider how much time you spend on the telephone listening to friends' problems or the latest gossip. How often are you reluctant to shorten a conversation for fear others will be offended? To test this, for one week make a record of the amount of time you spend on each phone conversation and note the subject of the conversation. The following week, try cutting your conversations by half. If friends have urgent problems, suggest professional assistance. This may prove more helpful to them.

Scheduling an alternative activity for the time usually devoted to telephone conversations may help you reduce telephone contacts without injuring feelings. You can anticipate some resentment when you shift, but you should take this as a clue that you are moving in the right direction. Ideally, you will learn to use the smallest increments of time and will soon find numerous ways in which to do it; thus you will become the master of your own time.

I am not advocating that you become an efficiency expert wedded to a rigid schedule. I am merely suggesting that you figure out what constitutes your most satisfying use of time and that you seek to increase that satisfaction by spending more time involved in that particular activity. As you recognize the value of even the smallest amounts of time, you may very well begin to organize your activities so as to reduce the confusion which often results from poor planning and disorganization of material which you now care for sloppily, so that you cannot find what you need when you want it.

Here, too, you may now find yourself discarding things you don't need, to increase your access to things you do need. In the long run this can save you an enormous amount of time.

B. Keep track of things you wish to do. Your memory is a storehouse of information about your characteristic approach to these issues. On the basis of past experience, consider habits you must continually work to overcome, situations to avoid, and successful approaches which can be further developed.

Do you have a tendency to be distracted and to forget what you were doing? Keep alert to habits that can reappear and impede your progress, such as the impulse to act before thinking. Consider what you wish to avoid doing on the basis of past experiences. For example, you may wish to avoid certain noxious or stressful situations, to avoid certain noxious people; excessive scheduling of activities is a bad habit which can lead to conflicts between two positive interests, making them negative interests for you. Develop those areas in which you have made decisions. These are areas of strength, and it makes sense to take up where you left off.

A review of previous experiences will assist you in avoiding time-consuming, unproductive activities. You can anticipate the recurring problems that have impeded progress in the past. Rather than rely on your memory, start keeping a diary, periodically reviewing it to determine regularities in your experience. This can be a valuable source of information about yourself, pointing out possible approaches to try, your tolerance point, sources of frustration in your past experiences, and the like.

C. Schedule your activities in advance, to facilitate efforts. In order to maximize the outcome, concentrate on the most important and most profitable things. Plan the first steps of an activity before starting. This will reduce inertia, friction, and confusion, and save time usually wasted wandering around in circles. If you shift your schedule, allow enough time for the shift so you won't feel rushed. Approach things directly, with systematic thought and a minimum of hesitation. To do this effectively, separate the decision-making period from the action or implementation stage. Decision-making and implementation require different mental attitudes. If you try to make decisions at the time of acting, indecision is likely.

D. Schedule several periods of free time each day for relaxation and self-renewal. The more absorbing the activity, the better the chance that relaxation will reduce residual preoccupations, tensions, and anxieties acquired during the day. Make a note of what you are doing so that you can resume your activity without delay.

E. Switch activities before you lose interest. Make a note of the specific step to return to.

F. Concentrate as much as possible on what you can do, and eliminate activities which frustrate or bore you. Avoid involvement in activities which are high priority for others and low priority for you.

Concentrate on your strengths and your interests. Don't be misguided by the flattery of others or the advice of those who may be responding to their own needs and thus may have a false concept of what you want.

Remember you can often get involved in low-priority activities to be courteous or agreeable even when you don't really want to do so.

G. Save time by modifying acceptable habits, not just by eliminating bad habits. Learn to skim newspaper headlines, reading only material of importance to you. For example, you can wait until tomorrow to read today's paper and wait until next year to read today's best-seller. Try modifying such simple but fixed routines as the 10:30 A.M. coffee break, the hour for lunch, or dinner at 6:00 P.M., to break out of the time restrictions of the past. This will give you a greater sense of mastery of time. Try the same with your sleep cycle, especially if you are a night owl and have been forcing yourself to sleep earlier than your body rhythm requires. Avoid standing in lines. If you can, go to work earlier or later to avoid the rush hour.

H. Save correspondence, bills, and other nonurgent or routine activities for slack periods, or until enough have accumulated to warrant the investment of time. Don't use your best hours for this routine work. In this way, you may be able to go through your letters and bills only once rather than repeatedly. Examine fixed routines which involve time, such as regular long chats and visits, and try this experiment. Skip the routine once without going into an elaborate explanation of what you are doing. Examine the feelings this gives you. How have others responded? Must you explain your reasons? The extent of your discomfort will show the extent to which such routines have become habits, as well as the extent to which your participation is not spontaneous or free.

I. Allow enough time for your activities to reduce the pressure of having insufficient time, which can lead you to sacrifice quality in what you do. Avoid time pressure, especially at certain hours of the day. Stretch out unimportant matters or put them off to a future date. Delegate the least important routines to others to have time for what you consider the most important priorities.

Philosophy of Life

Few things are impracticable in themselves. Most things fail not for want of means, but simply because of lack of application.

—*de la Rochefoucauld*

Unwillingness to actively seek self-reliance accounts for many failures. Fear of success rather than fear of failure probably accounts for this, since failure can be rationalized with a million excuses shared by others, some of whom may glorify failure as proof that they have rejected "materialism." Success connotes willingness to accept responsibility for your efforts. It does not mean accountability for results.

If you tend to blame your circumstances on someone or something other than yourself, you may not have realized that you alone determine your destiny through your own efforts. In fact, all you need concentrate on are your efforts, not the results. It would be tragic if you failed to realize that you have to concentrate only on the efforts you make, rather than on the results, to obtain satisfaction.

Whatever road you choose, you will learn about yourself if you pursue what you want most. If you refrain from acting until you have ascertained the responses of others, you have put your destiny into their hands. Pursue what you wish without regard for the outcome. The outcome will take care of itself, even in relationships with others. Here, too, concentrate on what you do, not on trying to control the results.

What you do determines results. Since your power results from your actions, not from the actions of others, you will not know what you can do until you try.

Do you focus on your weaknesses rather than your strengths, as so many do? Do you apologize for your efforts? Do you ask others to acknowledge the validity of your existence? Do you apologize for what you do in areas where you don't directly offend others? If so, you have been ignoring the basic human need to express your innermost drives.

People often prefer losing to winning, as if success violated the social need to conform to the group. Clearly, the difference between success and failure often depends on the degree of responsibility you are willing to accept.

Do you ask others to do things you can do yourself? Do you seek permission when you can act intuitively? According to Emerson, "The highest price to pay for something is to ask for it." Asking obligates you and diminishes your confidence in your decisions about what to do and how to do it, as if someone else knows enough about you to decide whether you can do what you want.

I do not mean to dispute the balance of nature. You must pay for what you want. Temporary failure may be the price. If it occurs, accept it and move on. The absence of failure suggests a minimum of effort, and the likelihood that little will be achieved. Failure thus represents genuine effort; it may be the next best thing to success. A famous gambler once said, "The next best thing to gambling and winning is gambling and losing."

Don't flaunt your success before others. Success results naturally from your efforts, not from your intrinsic value over others. Successful results indicate that you have adhered to the law of cause and effect. Since nature balances all things, your success will be balanced by failure and frustration. The ancients called this Nemesis, which, according to Emerson, meant that "in nature, nothing can be given, all things are sold." In nature's balance, you get nothing for nothing.

Emerson also said, "It is best to pay scot and lot as you go along." Pay as you go, for eventually you have to pay. You will pay for your failures as well, so it makes sense to stop avoiding success by trying to guarantee the outcome of your actions.

Your weakness may well be a source of strength. According to Emerson, "As no man had ever a point of pride that was not injurious to him, so no man had ever a defect that was not somewhere made useful to him." Remember, in every piece of adversity there is an equal or greater opportunity.

At times you may be distracted by supporters who praise your faults and ignore your strengths. In this sense, your critics may be your best source of information about yourself, and you should not ignore their observations. Consciously avoid the error of not accepting yourself, of trying to be what you are not, and of denying the good and exaggerating the bad in yourself, an attitude of self-abnegation frequently mistaken for humility.

True strength in a crisis requires patience, inner-directedness, postponement of action, and control of the automatic defensive responses, which often add to the turmoil of the crisis and make mastery of the situation difficult. Calmness fosters serenity and gives confidence to others as well. The strength to wait and act only when appropriate requires self-knowledge.

All things evolve in their own time, according to the law of cause and effect. Precipitous action may alter the direction of events and create new problems. Flow with events as they unravel and do not try to shape the future, for that can only generate crises and dilute your strength. There is no need to worry about unforeseen events or to feel guilty if events don't evolve exactly as you expect.

Begin new activities cautiously, with a minimum of discussion so as to avoid the unrealistic pessimism by others. This will give you greater freedom to decide on a course of action and will reduce the probability of conflicting mental images. Ideally, you should have only to concentrate on the situation's stimuli and your own automatic responses.

Keep alert at all times for the propitious moment to act, but keep in mind that by not acting you may have a powerful impact on events. Inaction may prevent you from complicating matters, and will give you a respite to recoup your strength. You cannot achieve everything at once, only slowly and perseveringly. At the moment of greatest distress, new solutions often appear, thus affecting a turnaround.

The notion of the meek inheriting the earth does not imply subservience, but rather a strategy for relating to dominating or threatening people. Meekness means gentleness and restraint in the face of attack, which in allowing an opponent to discharge his force weakens his domination. Fighting back against uneven odds when you are not prepared diverts energy and reduces the possibility that your opponent will wear himself out or overshoot the mark.

Knowing the right time for action requires experience. The impulsive must learn caution, the fearful boldness. An ideal combination consists of purposefulness with gentleness, friendliness, and adaptability.

How does this work? Emerson has pointed out that "the dice of God are always loaded." Accept your fate. Allow the law of compensation to work. This does not mean inaction, but only that you ought not to try to guarantee certain results. Concentrate only on your efforts to obtain the result. Your subconscious thoughts influence the outcome of events. Try to get in touch with this inner self and select the most desirable objectives, visualizing them and reviewing what you will do to achieve them. Then relax and go with it. Too much thought after programming yourself can spoil the results.

The power within you emerges through activity. The power of generating certain responses from others also results, consciously or unconsciously, from your actions. "Love and you shall be loved." We tend to evoke certain responses from others as a result of our own thoughts translated unconsciously into our facial expressions and body motions. Don't worry about what others may do to you. Keep calm and watch. Honest efforts cannot come to naught. Remember that your circumstances are only a reflection of your thoughts, conscious and unconscious.

In essence, follow your talents. Don't try to alter circumstances to guarantee results. You need only create the appropriate climate for the natural expression of your inner abilities, and the results will take care of themselves. You need not conform to what others claim will guarantee results, since eventually you will find a level suited to you. The extra effort of acting against your grain will have proved frustrating and distracting.

Everything develops in its own time. Go slowly.

Reviewing your past experiences may help you to find your special stamp, your unique qualities. Your memory can assist you to find your gifts. In the end, you must trust your intuition about your abilities and talent. Pursue these goals honestly and without compromise. You need not apologize for a slow start or an imperfect performance. Don't be distracted by attention showered on others. The price for envy can be high.

Jog your memory, examine your daydreams and dreams. Prepare for the day when you will have the chance to express your talents. Select your activities, your friends, and everything else in terms of your own criteria.

Don't be trapped by pretending to be other than you are because you think that others expect you to be different or because you don't measure up to your notion of their standards. Don't apologize for yourself. Don't conceal your strengths out of embarrassment, or focus on your weaknesses. Accept yourself as you are. Indeed, if you concentrate on your strengths, you need not even consider your weaknesses. Ultimately, your time is of value and you are of value and you should not force yourself to change simply to conform to some idealized standards.

A goal will generate the vitality within you. If you become absorbed in the present, you will lose the social mask you may have acquired as a defense against the opinions of others and will discover much greater personal satisfaction and wisdom. The more you can rely on yourself to accomplish something, the greater will be your satisfaction and the fewer will be your worries about what others think or do. Thus, whatever you do, you will do best at what is most important for you. The emphasis is not so much on thinking as on appreciation of the validity of what you do. Only you can know your innermost goals and the path to take. Keeping things to yourself will give you an extra dynamism which may have charismatic effects on others. Don't explain yourself; simply do and let others learn what you are doing by your actions. This may inspire them. Emerson has noted that "every heroic act measures itself by its contempt of some external good." Whatever you decide to do may have to be done in opposition to the views of others. Expecting this, you can bypass it by not asking whether or not you can do something, but by staying within the law and acting honestly. This is true in job situations, where people rarely recognize how wide the latitude is. Generally, people are acting in a more restrained way than is necessary for the given organization or situation. Have no fear of others' scorn, ridicule, or criticism. Avoid pettiness. "If you do good," said Emerson, "you put God in your debt."

Remember, too, that while the goal may activate you, achieving it will not be sufficient to vitalize your life. You must then seek another goal. Remember also that good and bad have a common cause and that there is a balance in results. You need only continue your efforts when you are getting bad results. The good results will surely follow. Confucius is said to have noted: "Danger arises when a man feels secure in his position. Destruction threatens when a man seeks to preserve his worldly estate. Confusion develops when a man has put everything in order. Therefore, the superior man does not forget danger in his security, nor ruin when he is well established, nor confusion when his affairs are in order. In this way, he gains personal safety and is able to protect the empire."

Conscious and rational decision-making should apply to the selection of your way of life. Comfort induces laziness and increases distraction and illusory notions of yourself, fostering distorted perceptions others may have of you.

The law of compensation applies to the balance between good and evil and to the link between advantages and disadvantages. Perfection and permanent happiness are unrealistic objectives. In accepting a new position, you lose the prerogatives of the previous position. In fear of losing something, you may seek to preserve the status quo, but in doing this you also do not gain any prerogatives. Holding on too tightly retards growth and advancement, and inhibits the full flowering of your potential. New activities provide vehicles for freeing yourself.

If you wish to succeed, concentrate on what you can do. Expanding your efforts into other activities will dilute your power to achieve your goals. Strength supported by faith in the future develops from patience, knowing that your turn will come. If you know what to do with power, it will come to you. Until then, don't grasp for it too quickly, for you will only burn your hands.

Remember that love may be the strongest kind of power in the world. Don't hesitate to share your efforts with others. Don't worry about whether they will copy you.

What you give, you receive. Since action and reaction are equal, you keep what you give away. You will be enriched by giving of yourself, not by giving with the expectation of return.

Checklist for Unscrambling Your Life

1. Look for situations where you differ from popular opinion. Consider what you may have done for others who have called you "crazy." Imagine alternative opinions to the ones you had. Try shifting your routines—delay your response in routine situations. Buy your food and paper at a new store for a week. Try a new parking space. Reduce your phone calls by half an hour. Practice letting the phone ring three more times than usual.

2. Compare your gut reactions to your rationalizations for inactivity. Conversely, observe your rationalization of activity, as when a situation demands action and you make an effort to flow with it despite your inner urgings.

3. Observe how often others think they know what is best for you. How often do you allow others to plan for you or take care of needs you can handle yourself? This is demonstrated when one visits friends and relatives and

makes an effort to please people by courteously accepting what they provide even if it is inconvenient.

4. Observe how often you seek permission before trying something and how often you try to determine the reactions of others to what you plan to do. This sometimes takes the form of trying to determine the attitudes or customs of others, customs which may differ from your own; an example of this would be to do something in a situation where you can make the judgment as to whether it's okay or not.

5. Keep notes on the number of apologies you make in a given day. Do you regularly apologize for the same thing? Do you apologize for asking a favor, thereby denying the other person the opportunity to feel generous? Are there specific people to whom you regularly apologize?

6. Keep track of how much time you spend on the here and now. Do you catch up on old tasks instead of transferring them to someone else or discarding them? Do you try to manipulate the future, so that spontaneous interests become chores?

7. How often do you boast about your failures to others, as if to mask an underlying sense of superiority? Do you fear that people will criticize you for being immodest? Are you afraid to refer to your successes?

8. How much time do you spend creating impressions about yourself? When you meet new people, do you start boasting about yourself defensively, or are you silent out of fear instead of exploring common interests? Do you become concerned when people fail to acknowledge you, or do you take too seriously the defense of people who

praise you? Keep track of the extent to which you multiply your activities to create an impression or to assert yourself in ways that conflict with the image others have of you.

9. Increase the time you spend at home by reducing participation in activities which no longer interest you. Don't rush into new activities. Those who have time to kill seek to share it with you and then box you in with their urgency to prove themselves. Be conscious of situations where you are pressed into activities that others think will interest you. Have your own objectives and involve those who wish to help you in your activities. In this way you can activate new and unfamiliar interests. Don't wait for someone to determine what you can and cannot do. Implement your own plans. Critical information will be forthcoming. You need not feel you must be busy with someone else's plans for you.

10. Don't flaunt your success. Focus instead on your work, and you will be less concerned with the trappings of success; you will also worry less about the opinions of others, a concern which can become all-consuming. Control can be difficult in periods of crisis or change. Weigh your capabilities before entering new areas.

11. Reduce regularities in your associations which may distract you from new aims. Spend more time at home. Take courses. Read. Be alert to the traps you create by feeling obliged to continue activities which helped you build your reputation or success. Search alone for new aims. In new places, try out sides of yourself which new people may be willing to accept. Through self-control, try to minimize the habitual. Don't be afraid to lose yourself in new interests. Don't be too eager for results. Let them emerge; your efforts will always lead to results, although you may not recognize the results if they are not what you were ex-

pecting. Since everything in the world already exists, you need only find your own solution. Through effort, your hidden potential will expand and reach its fullest expression. Natural, unspoken acts reflect this hidden potential best, although it will show through disguises as well.

Select stresses you can master, learning to control your responses to external events. People who succeed sometimes become dependent on the external rewards and often lose sight of the sources of their greatest satisfaction.

12. Calculate the time you now spend in solitude, and for the next thirty days, try to spend a few moments alone at the same time every day, contemplating what has been going on that day, before resuming your activity. Such periods of solitude provide opportunity for self-renewal.

13. Remember, "here is best." The critical time for accomplishing anything is in the here and now. Don't bring preconceptions about your limits into solutions. Evaluate the present with its possibilities. Explore the task of cooperating with and motivating others. To do this, you must first decide on those areas for which you can and should assume responsibility and those for which you should relinquish responsibility. Redefine what you can do for others and what they can do themselves—helping them by not becoming involved in their efforts. Consider how often you assume responsibility for others because of a desire to be appreciated, to be a martyr, and to "do good." At times, to do nothing may make perfect sense. Consider the interests and potentials of others and areas of activity where your unique strengths can be combined and can work synergistically rather than antagonistically.

14. You can influence people through their own thoughts by evoking in them an awareness of their own uniqueness and sense of self-esteem. You can do this by seeking the

special perspectives of others, asking questions rather than giving answers. Discern how an individual's remarks relate to what else he has said. These steps relate to "the best listeners"—those who pursue pertinent questions, not those who talk too much.

15. Don't try to control others through excessive efforts to help. Don't try to predict the future for others, which can influence the outcome by fostering fear of errors or over-confidence and reduced effort. This also sets limits on situations and fails to recognize the power in each new moment and the unpredictability of the world. The out-come exists, although you may not know it yet. Act on faith, allowing things to evolve.

16. Quiet contemplation and observation of others may help you see how much responsibility they can all assume for their activities, reducing the urgency to act right away. Most often, assuming responsibility for others will trap you, producing resentment, frustration, and sometimes even an explosion of hostility. More important, not assuming re-sponsibilities which you have always assumed for others will lead them to assume responsibility for themselves.

17. Remember, you don't have to do anything that you don't want to do, nor do you have to explain yourself to others or justify your existence. Don't worry when others tease you or express eagerness to undertand you in order to help you. Learn how to keep confidences—not only others', but your own as well.

18. Generally, movement toward your goals will stimulate others to follow. Don't be authoritarian, ordering others to act in certain ways, which can frustrate you and prevent them from learning. Movement toward a goal will give you a sense of your center and give others confidence in

you, since you will appear certain, and others will find it easier to empathize with you.

People are drawn by spiritual attractions. You need not search others out; they will find you. As Emerson observed: "Whenever a feeling is voiced with truth and frankness, whenever a deed is the clear expression of sentiment, a mysterious and far-reaching influence is exerted. . . . The root of all influence lies in one's own inner being. Given true and vigorous expression in word and deed, the effect is great. You need only concentrate on the causes. The results will occur." The effect is but the reflection of something that emanates from one's own heart. Any deliberate intention to produce an effect would only destroy the possibility of producing it. To encourage others to follow you, remember that simple actions can be more easily imitated.

19. Be especially cautious before reaching a goal. During stress periods be cautious about trying too hard to advance. Go slowly, with your goals in mind. The ability to postpone your reactions to external stimuli will increase your inner strength and mastery of events. Things generally evolve in accord with their original directions. The closer development relates to these original directions, the less effort is involved.

20. A low profile averts negative responses. This reduces the distraction which comes from the additional expectations of others, and makes it possible for your performance to relate to your expectations. In times of stress, try to understand the demands of the moment. A spirit of humility and cooperation while asserting your prerogatives is desirable. Pace yourself so as not to overshoot the mark. When you achieve a goal, don't relax and slip into old patterns. Start projects cautiously, maintaining a balance. Be cautious of the tendency to try to win favor or to look good if you

don't have the support of the people in power. Remember, you cannot lose the power you have; it will develop in time. Use the situation to develop the necessary support by seeking it in yourself.

21. Don't look back at dangers you have averted, lest you fall into them. Pursue your course without looking sidewise so as to retain the inner freedom that will help you to move forward.

In essence, what I have sought to outline in this book are some of the critical dimensions of various life situations defining relevant boundaries and underscoring areas of behavior which can be changed to give you greater control over your life.

Each of us possesses characteristics of the universe within ourselves. If you act in terms of your true nature, you can shape your future. Your self-concept relates to your true nature. Give expression to your potential for good. Intellect, will, wisdom, and action are the critical elements. If your thoughts and actions exist in harmony, your emotional reactions will be harmonious. The more you comprehend the nature of events around you and function in accordance with them, the greater will be your ability to master your own fate.